Studies in Robertson Davies' Deptford Trilogy

Edited by Robert G. Lawrence and Samuel L. Macey
With an Introductory Essay by Robertson Davies

English Literary Studies
University of Victoria

1980

ENGLISH LITERARY STUDIES

Published at the University of Victoria

ISBN 0-920604-38-2

The ELS Monograph Series is published in consultation with members of the Department by ENGLISH LITERARY STUDIES, Department of English, University of Victoria, B.C., Canada.

ELS Monograph Series No. 20

CONTENTS

PREFACE

In September 1978 we cast a large net into the Canadian academic sea, hoping to make a substantial Deptford catch. We could not anticipate exactly what we might bring in, but we were delighted with the enthusiastic response; several students of the trilogy nibbled, and—the metaphor must not become too painful—we had a modest flood of submissions. Our craft was not large enough to accept all of them.

It is obviously a tribute to Robertson Davies that our invitation attracted such a variety of essays about the Deptford trilogy. Those which appear here are all different in their approach to the essential subject and show surprisingly little overlapping or contradiction. The contributors were, of course, writing in isolation from one another, and even though we did not agree with every statement that they made, we have resisted the temptation to tamper with content.

The order of essays between the covers suggested itself: Professor Davies looks back to the conception of the Deptford trilogy; Professor Radford considers the relationship between Robertson Davies' earlier Salterton trilogy (1952-58) and *Fifth Business*; three contributors examine three different aspects of the later Deptford trilogy: folklore, time, and the public figure; two writers concentrate on biographical and Jungian themes in *Fifth Business* (1970); two focus on the archaeological and legal backgrounds of *The Manticore* (1972); and the last essay concerns itself with one of the novelist's major interests in *World of Wonders* (1975).

We wish to thank the scholar-contributors who live between Vancouver and St. John's, friends and colleagues who helped with advice, our patient wives, and, above all, Professor Robertson Davies, the only begetter, who responded generously to our request for a short introductory essay. We hope that these papers will send readers back to the Deptford trilogy with greater appreciation and understanding.

R.G.L.
S.L.M.

University of Victoria

The Deptford Trilogy in Retrospect

Robertson Davies

It was not my intention to write three novels about the story that forms the basis for what people now call the Deptford trilogy. I had only one book in mind, and its character was unlike any of those which were finally written. How unlike, I was reminded when recently I discovered some notes I had made, certainly not later than 1960. If anyone is interested, here they are:

> In a small town a young parson is taking his pregnant wife for an evening walk: a mischievous boy throws a snowball in which there is a stone; hits the woman on the head, hurting her seriously. When the child is born prematurely she loses her reason: after a period of care at home, she is sent to an asylum.

> N.B.: though seemingly strong, the parson is v. dependent on his wife: his reluctance to send her to an asylum is as much this as it is concern for her: he needs her not simply as a woman to care for him (neighbour women do that) but he must have this particular woman: what seems to the romantic to be love is also extreme psychological thralldom, for in her he has idealized all womanhood.

> When she has to be put away he "goes to pieces" and at last has to be replaced as parson: new parson v. good to him but feels him as a weight. Particularly so as, relieved of his clerical duties, he becomes "queer" and talks of revenge.

> *Revenge* is the theme of the novel; is revenge practicable in such circumstances? Not for the parson: he cannot bring himself to it.

> But he urges it upon his son & the son comes to attribute all that is wrong in his life to the boy who "killed" his mother & caused his premature birth.

> But how can it be accomplished?

> Does father become a small-town occultist?

> Examine small-town spiritualism and superstition.

> The rotting effect of second-rate belief and quackery.

> Son decides that murder is not the answer: brings only a ruined life. But begins to haunt his enemy, seeking to destroy him.

7

Is the enemy fortunate? Is this a story of the inequality of human destiny —the Fated? Can revenge be the mainspring of a life & can it lead to any real fulfilment?

Narrator: a small-town editor's son, 1st Gt. War veteran & now a master in a private school.

I was not able to write the novel for several years after I made these notes. I was busy changing myself from a newspaper editor into a professor and organizing a college at the University of Toronto. But in 1968 I turned again to the novel.

While lying wherever it had been at the back of my mind it had undergone important changes. During the intervening years I had been occupied, in my few leisure hours, with problems of guilt. Where did it arise? At what age was a human creature capable of feeling and assuming the burden of guilt? Were the truly guilty always as burdened as were those whose up-bringing and moral training disposed them to feel guilt and perhaps also to assume guilt which was not truly theirs? The novel, when I began to write it, was about guilt, and not revenge, though revenge played some part in it.

When the book appeared, first of all, in Canada, I was wryly amused by its reception. Canadian reviewers on the whole did not like it, and a few of them seemed almost affronted by what they thought of as a change in my tone. I had been, they said, a comic novelist, and they gave their readers to understand that a comic novelist was not a very considerable creature. I could have said to them, in Dr. Johnson's words, that "it was bitterness which they mistook for frolick," but I do not suppose they would have understood. The seriousness of *Fifth Business* showed an instability in my character of which they could not approve. One of them referred to me as "an old-timer" who seemed to have quitted the field of novel-writing and was now seeking to make a comeback. I was in my fifties and it had not occurred to me that I was wholly spent as a writer; indeed, most of the writers I most admired had done their best work when youth was well and truly past.

When the book appeared in the U.S. it was received with flattering enthusiasm and this again was so puzzling to some Canadian reviewers that one of them, from a very large newspaper, actually visited me and asked me how I accounted for it. His paper had not found the book to be of more than very ordinary quality, and here were American critics disagreeing, as though the Canadian edict had not gone out. What did I make of it?

What I made of it was that several American writers had asked to hear more about the characters in *Fifth Business* and as a professional writer, eager to please a new public, I was ready to satisfy them, if I could. So I wrote *The Manticore*.

To do so I had to solve a technical difficulty of substantial proportions. I had told the story of the boy who felt most guilty for the unlucky flight of that snowball, and I wanted to write about the boy who had actually thrown it, and who had succeeded in avoiding any feeling of guilt whatever. But to write the story of an extravert and egotist in the first person did not appeal to me, and I decided to write it from the point of view of his son, who was compelled, as children often are, to live out the unlived portion of his father's life and to be driven to an unwanted recognition of the kind of man his father truly was. How? I recall the day and the place when it came to me that it might be done by putting the son into a Jungian analysis, during which the truth might be painfully extracted from him and the recognition made inevitable.

This was tricky work, for the full story of an analysis would be intolerably extended and tedious, and I had Jungian friends who would be watching me for any falsities or misrepresentations. But I telescoped the analytical work into a single year, and I am proud that many learned Jungians have thought it well managed.

Of course the reviewers were quick to point out what they considered an excessive dependence on coincidence in the novel—a complaint they had also made about *Fifth Business*. But I decided that it must be that reviewers are less subject to coincidence than are novelists. Or it could be that my Jungian studies had inclined me to be more observant of coincidence than they. A small instance may serve as illustration; after *Fifth Business* I was sought out by the New York *Times* writer, Israel Shenker, who wished to know if I had been in extensive correspondence with the Bollandist Fathers? I had described them as writing with steel pens in purple ink, which he knew to be the case; how had I known that? The answer was that I had not known it, but it seemed likely. Coincidence? Or a lucky guess? But when *The Manticore* appeared it was insisted by several Jungians who knew her personally that I had drawn my analyst, in appearance and manner, from one of the most famous of Dr. Jung's pupils and a noted Zürich analyst, Dr. Marie-Louise von Franz. But at that time I had never met Dr. von Franz nor had I read much of her work. Very soon afterwards I did meet her; she had not been pleased with the reports that she had been made use of in a book by a writer of whom she had never heard. But when she read the novel we agreed that coincidence had been at work sufficiently to deceive a number of readers, though she insisted, "I am most certainly not that woman." Nor was she.

9

These things seem not to happen in the lives of reviewers.

If I appear to be paying too much attention to the opinions of reviewers, I should say that reviews are the first response an author receives to his book, at a time when he is more than ordinarily sensitive; later, when letters began to reach me from readers, I found that they had accepted the books in the spirit in which I wrote them, and the warmth of their approval was very gratifying to me. An author learns the public's opinion of his work slowly, and long after most of the reviews, good or bad, have been forgotten.

After *The Manticore*, reviewers and my publishers in the States were anxious for more, and I rounded out the story by telling it once again, and from the point of view of Paul Dempster, in *World of Wonders*. I particularly enjoyed writing this book because in it I was able to include a description of a theatrical tour across Canada, a cultural phenomenon of my childhood and youth, and one of the things that gave the country, at that time, some semblance of cultural unity. Nobody had done it before, and I thought it significant. In our present atmosphere of super-heated and often factitious nationalism we are sometimes reluctant to admit that not very long ago we were culturally a colony, not only of Great Britain, but of the U.S., and that very few people saw anything wrong with that state of affairs— that, indeed, it had a positive side. Canada, as the travelling players saw it, and Canada, as it saw the travelling players, seems to me to be the authentic stuff of romance.

I had dealt with the three principal characters in the complex of events that was brought about by the unlucky flight of a snowball, and I had no more to say. Many people have asked me to write the story of one of the women who figures in the books, the millionairess Liesl Vitzliputzli, but I feel no impulse to do so. Too much explanation of such a character would be a great mistake, and beside, Liesl was not present when the story began, as were the three men.

Since then the three novels have been widely read in many countries, and have been commented upon by a variety of critics who have discovered in them meanings that surprised me, but which I do not say have no validity. A book of any value, as we all know from our university days, must first of all be a story, must provide some substance of allegory, and must say something about the condition of man which readers are either willing to accept as true, or to which they are prepared to give serious attention. The story of the trilogy is plain enough: a happening which is only in part an accident sets in motion a train of incidents that strongly influence the lives of three men, and each man's personality determines the way in which he accepts what comes to him. To one it brings revelation; to another disillusionment and death; to the third wealth, fame and revenge.

The allegorical element in the story is for others to discover and determine. Some critics have written admirably about the trilogy, responding to it like artists of another sort, and I have been grateful for what they have said—and not merely because it makes me seem cleverer than I really am. The truth is that I would rather not explore these allegorical avenues myself, because I have a conviction that a writer is in a dangerous frame of mind when he thinks of himself as an allegorist—unless of course he sets out with the fixed intention of writing something which is primarily allegorical. If his story is a good one, if it has artistic validity, the allegory will be inherent in it, but woe betide him if he begins to be too much aware of the allegory while he is writing.

These books have been extensively read in schools and many of the teachers seem to be bears for allegory. They, and their pupils, write to me and sometimes they use a form of words that puzzles me. "What you are really trying to say is . . ." they write, and then they tell me about their allegorical explanation. But writers are vain creatures; I think I have said what I intended to say in the clearest terms I could find, and I do not think their explanations greatly clarify anything, because they have not troubled with the third element in the story, which is some comment on the nature of life. As I have already said, I think of coincidence as a powerful element in life, as is also the operation of destiny, which may or may not be blind, but which is unquestionably powerful. This does not make me a thorough-going determinist, but certainly I mean to suggest that the forces that shape a man's fate are not wholly under his control, because some of them reside in that part of his psyche that depth-psychologists call the Unconscious. As one of the wisest men I have had the good fortune to know once said to me, we attract what we are. Whatsoever a man soweth, that shall he also reap. The lifelong task is to learn what we are, and what we are sowing because of it.

Another question I am often asked is whether the books are meant to present an interpretation of life in Canada. Of course they are, for all the three principal characters are Canadians, one of whom has been shaped by Canada's unquestioned virtues, but also by its want of spiritual self-recognition; the second, exposed to the same virtues, yields to Canada's allurements of glossy success; the third feels the lash of Canada's cruelty, which is the shadow side of its virtues, and arises from Canada's lack of self-knowledge. Neither the virtues nor the shadows are solely Canadian;

11

they are universal, but in Canada they bear the authentic Made in Canada mark.

The temptation to continue is strong, but I must not yield to it, because writers more skilled than I in this sort of exposition have written the essays that make up the contents of this book.

MASSEY COLLEGE
UNIVERSITY OF TORONTO

The Apprentice Sorcerer: Davies' Salerton Trilogy

F. L. Radford

If one returns to Robertson Davies' first three novels after reading the Deptford trilogy it is easy to see them as preliminary exercises in the development of certain themes and motifs that are brought to mature expression in the later works. There is a particularly close connection between the Salterton trilogy and *Fifth Business,* as if the first novel of the Deptford trilogy resolves some of Davies' earlier concerns while opening the way for *The Manticore* and *World of Wonders.* In the two earliest novels the shared elements appear in retrospect as the fragmented announcement of themes before they are fully developed in a symphony. A fuller development is attempted with imperfect success in *A Mixture of Frailties,* and development and resolution are achieved in *Fifth Business* and its sequels, after a maturing pause of twelve years.

The theme of the revenge of the unlived life, expressed in Dunstan Ramsay as the self-controlled teacher whose passions explode in middle-aged infatuation for the young Faustina, is prefigured in a parodic way by Hector Mackilwraith of *Tempest-Tost.* Mackilwraith is also a teacher and his character has also been shaped by a Scots Presbyterian upbringing in an Ontario village. He shares Ramsay's dourness of appearance and is given the nickname of "Saint Andrew" because of his "solemn and silent" manner. As a boy, he savagely defends his mother against what he regards as a sexual innuendo and is punished, not so much for beating the boy who made the remark as for refusing to explain his action to the school principal—he cannot speak of sexual matters to an adult. In middle age, given the role of Gonzago in the amateur production of *The Tempest* which provides the novel with an allusive pattern, Hector falls desperately in love with the young woman who plays Ariel and becomes in real life an inarticulate Caliban to her Miranda. Spying on her in helpless devotion, he observes her embracing Roger Tasset, the Ferdinand of the play and a superficial Don Juan who remotely prefigures the Boy Staunton of *Fifth Business.* In passionate despair, Hector fails in a comic attempt to hang himself and achieves his own limited apotheosis in awaking solus in his beloved's bed and later being pityingly comforted by her.

But Mackilwraith is more of a case history than a character and the resemblances to Ramsay merely point up the growth of Davies' art in *Fifth Business*. As a teacher, Hector is a competent bully, lacking Ramsay's individuality and complexity. As "Saint Andrew" he has none of the richness of Ramsay's saint-obsession or his role of confessor/priest to Staunton. The fight over his mother's reputation has none of the depth of Ramsay's defence of Mary Dempster in the face of his own mother's prohibition and the duality which so richly explores the nature of the mother image and its variations. Hector's infatuation for Griselda, complicated by the rivalry of Tasset, is the focus of the novel, but does not carry farther than Ramsay's rivalry with Boy Staunton over Leola. It lacks entirely the extra dimensions given to Ramsay's Faustina infatuation by Eisengrim's illusion of Faust torn between sacred and profane love, by Ramsay's discovery of Liesl as a female rival for Faustina's affections, or by the replacement of Faustina in Ramsay's own affections by the demonic Liesl with the increased self-knowledge that relationship brings.

Ramsay as the son tormented by the demon-mother who demands absolute loyalty is paralleled in all three Salterton novels by Solly Bridgetower, whose possessive mother is described as both saint and devil and "both pitiable and terrible."[1] Solly says that she "is enough to warn me off the female sex for life."[2] She fights any attempt of her son to escape, and when Solly does marry Veronica Vambrace they must live with his mother. In *A Mixture of Frailties*, the dead hand of Mrs. Bridgetower reaches melodramatically out of the grave in a last effort to destroy her son's marriage through a will requiring a male child before Solly can inherit her large estate. We are even given to understand that the first boy child is stillborn because he has been strangled in the womb by the spirit of Mrs. Bridgetower, which haunts the house. In *Fifth Business*, this literal revenge is transformed into more subtle psychological after-effects as the dead hand of the possessive mother shapes Ramsay's perceptions of other women, superimposing her image upon them and preventing him from forming a fruitful union.

The comforting mother appears in *Leaven of Malice* as Mrs. Fielding, who accepts the confession of Mr. Ridley and relieves him of a twenty-year burden of guilt and secrecy. Ridley's wife has been in an asylum for twenty years and he has visited her regularly though she has not recognized him for the last fifteen years. He feels guilty for her state because it may have resulted from a car accident which happened while they were quarrelling and because he had wished her dead many times. The seeds are here for

Mary Dempster's madness and Ramsay's guilt over the stone in the snowball, but the difference between Mrs. Fielding's image of beautiful woman as mother-confessor and Liesl as the recipient and judge of Ramsay's confessions typifies the development between the two novels. Mrs. Fielding lightens Ridley's burden by unspecified advice, none of which is "extraordinarily wise, or uncommonly deep" but all of which is "rooted fast in love and womanly tenderness."[3] By contrast, Ramsey gains wisdom and "healing tenderness" from Liesl only after he has wrestled with her as an embodiment of the demon-woman, so that Davies succeeds in uniting in her the fearsome and comforting sides of the mother image.

The three early novels have many other premonitions of later themes and motifs, but the novels are also characterized by incompleteness of development and flatness of statement in comparison to the more satisfying treatment in the Deptford trilogy. In *Leaven of Malice*, Pearl Vambrace tells Solly that she also has "a saint's name . . . Veronica."[4] This is at the point where she is to become his wife and ally against the devouring mother and where he is to rescue her from her domineering father. She now takes the saint's name as her usual Christian name. In *A Mixture of Frailties*, there is a question of Monica Gall taking a professional name as a singer, and the Dean remarks, "I've sometimes thought we might all be the better for taking new names when we discover our vocations."[5] There are suggestions here of the major theme of name and identity and the "twice-born" in the later trilogy. In Solly's mind, the "saint" and his mother struggle for dominance in a curious scene in which he lies awake in his room thinking, "Veronica; as Veronica she seemed to be someone quite new"—while his mother lies awake in her room below; his thoughts continue:

> How easy, how utterly simple, for Solly to turn back to Mother—to drive away the powerful but still strange vision of Veronica, and to give himself to Mother forever! Should he run down the stairs and into her room *now*, to kiss her, and tell her that he would be her little boy forever? Thus life and death warred in Solly's bosom in the night, and in her bedroom his mother lay, yearning for him, willing him to come to her.[6]

In the later *Fifth Business*, this struggle is transformed into the much more fully developed conflict amongst Mary Dempster, as saint, and Ramsay's mother as possessive demon, and the influence of their respective images on his relationships with women throughout his life.

In *Leaven of Malice*, we also have the beginnings of the Fifth Business idea of the small action that widens out to affect the lives of many people. In this case it is the spurious announcement of the engagement of Solly and Pearl which throws them together and leads to their real engagement. The idea is more extensively explored in *A Mixture of Frailties* where Mrs. Bridge-tower's will, designed solely to plague Solly and Veronica, has profound effects on the lives of people she has never known—Monica Gall and her family and all those she meets as a result of the unexpected bequest that enables her to study in England. This novel is generally more fully developed than the first two, which seem very thin in comparison with *Fifth Business*. Davies himself, with more-or-less tongue in cheek, has described them more than once as "trivial and jejune productions."[7] The part of *A Mixture of Frailties* that is placed amongst the Bridgetower set in Salterton remains largely on the level of mild social satire characteristic of *Tempest-Tost* and *Leaven of Malice*, but the bulk of the novel—the part concerned with the psyche of Monica Gall—can be seen as an important trial run for *Fifth Business* and the Deptford trilogy. With this third novel, Davies' concerns and character creation deepen as they centre on what is to become a key theme of the later novels: the Canadian in Europe, discovering unexpected psychic roots in the older culture and faced with the need to decide how much of that culture and its manners must be absorbed for true self-understanding but without total loss of independent identity. In the complex of characters that includes Monica Gall, Dunstan Ramsay, Magnus Eisen-grim, Boy Staunton and David Staunton, Davies seems to argue that a full flowering of the graft of Canadian culture requires that the European roots be watered but that those roots are always ready to send forth their own shoots to overcome the young and vulnerable Canadian stock. Thus, at the end of *Mixture*, Monica Gall stands poised between an English and a Canadian identity. For a large part of *Fifth Business*, Boy Staunton makes himself into an ersatz English gentleman. Paul Dempster, as Faustus Legrand and later as Eisengrim, becomes a European. Set against this pattern in *Mixture* are the Canadian couple, Lorne and Meg McCorkell, who live in England behind a barricade of North American appliances and food, desperately repelling attacks by the older culture. But in all the novels the figures most closely allied in their experiences are Monica Gall and Dunstan Ramsay, although her acquisition of professional skill in England is closer to the experience of Paul Dempster in *World of Wonders*.

In learning her art as a singer, Monica is also carried back through her unknown artistic heritage to its classical roots. On a visit to Paris after a quarrel with her lover, she has a moment of intense devotion and awe at the tomb of Saint Geneviève and prays for help from the saint whose presence seems to remain with her afterwards. Like Ramsay, then, Monica goes from Canada to polish her manners and find her sexual initiation in England and to discover a new and more personal religious consciousness in Europe, but

16

her abrupt and truncated revelation at the tomb of St. Geneviève is a rather unconvincing preview of Ramsay's vision on the battlefield. By giving the numinous image of the Virgin Mother the face of Mary Dempster, Davies is able to integrate Ramsay's religious experience with the central themes of *Fifth Business*. In *Mixture*, he does not yet seem entirely at ease with the religious subjects that he wishes to deal with. Monica's religious experience seems to be superimposed on the novel, as is the case with the rather heavily underlined lectures by the fatherly Sir Benedict Domdaniel on the subjects of Eros and Thanatos and the meaning of life in general. Though we are told that the saint remains important to Monica, her discovery does not lead on to the kind of self-aware exploration of the nature of religion that takes Ramsay from his battlefield vision to his identification with Saint Dunstan and on to a recognition of myth and legend as instrinsic elements of history and the individual human life.

A Mixture of Frailties also marks an important advance in Davies' use of Jungian concepts of the human psyche for the creation of characters with depth and variety. The characters of the first two novels are quite one-dimensional—even the explosion of passion in Hector Mackilwraith and the change in character of Pearl Vambrace are merely plot-governed reversals. Monica Gall remains essentially the same character from beginning to end of *A Mixture of Frailties*, but what we see is the unfolding of the possibilities of that character to us and to herself. It is a working out of Ramsay's comment that people have not two, but twenty-two sides to them. When Giles Revelstoke's opera of *The Golden Asse* is performed, in *Mixture*, it is called an allegory "disclosing the metamorphosis of life itself, in which man moves from confident inexperience through the bitterness of experience, towards the rueful wisdom of self-knowledge."[8] This is said in Davies' own voice as narrator and it might well serve as an epigraph for the later trilogy, as well as being an adumbration of Jung's pattern of the stages of life. Shortly after the appearance of *A Mixture of Frailties*, Davies said in his collection of essays, *A Voice from the Attic*, that "Dr. Jung's approach to the obscure places of the mind by means of depth psychology seems to work better for people who have passed the age of forty than the uncompromising Freudian method."[9] This certainly seems to be true for Davies as a writer.

In Monica Gall, the Jungian character pattern which is so strong in the Deptford trilogy is first fully apparent. Curiously, her very name suggests the town of St. Gall which figures so importantly in Davies' most overtly Jungian novel, *The Manticore*. In view of the heavily masculine emphasis of the Deptford trilogy, it is interesting that Davies' first clearly Jungian protagonist should be a woman. This may have something to do with the fact that the work that first gave Jung's ideas widespread distribution in English, *Psychology of the Unconscious,* is built around the psycho-analytic case history of a woman. In the revised version of that work, now entitled *Symbols of Transformation,* Jung describes the "products of the unconscious" that consist of "archetypal structures which coincide with the myth-motifs, among them certain types which deserve the name of dominants. These are archetypes like the anima, animus, wise old man, witch, shadow, earth-mother, etc., and the organizing dominants, the self, the circle, and the quaternity, i.e., the four functions or aspects of the self or of consciousness."[10] Many of Jung's "dominant" archetypes are present in both *A Mixture of Frailties* and *Fifth Business.* The mother archetype is everywhere and is as important to Monica as it is to Ramsay. Of course, one of the basic differences between Freud and Jung is that for the latter the Oedipus Complex is an archetype that is simply one of many and that the mother archetype can be as important for a woman as for a man. All of Ramsay's women partake in some degree of this image and in *Mixture* there is also a complex of mothers. Mrs. Bridgetower is a possessive demon to Solly, a witch to Veronica, and a good fairy to Monica. The mother of Monica's lover, the rather weakly demonic composer, Giles Revelstoke, contributes to his death through her failure to understand or support his work. Monica's own mother is described as a "failed artist" and as the "earth mother" and "the Many-Breasted Mother" and she is in her own way as dominant in Monica's early life as Ramsay's mother is in his. Monica's father is even more of a shadowy consort than is Ramsay's. Sir Benedict Domdaniel becomes a substitute father and wise old man figure, as Padre Blazon does for Ramsay, but lacking the marvellously economical vitality of the Blazon character. Persis Kinwellmarshe is a witch and shadowy figure for Monica's psyche, showing on the one hand the possibility of freed sexuality and on the other the danger of existing only for that function.

As the principal animus figure—the female soul projected into a male image—Giles Revelstoke is a counterpart of several of Ramsay's female, anima, figures. A weak man who stages a suicide when he feels himself rejected, he prefigures Leola in *Fifth Business.* As a possessive lover who initiates Monica into the mysteries of sex and who teaches her how to mix with London sophisticates, he has some of the functions of Diana Manners. More than Domdaniel or Molloy, Monica's other teachers, Giles is influential in freeing her from the limitations of family and background. As a guide into the darker self-knowledge, he is the animus in demonic guise, as Liesl is for Ramsay, and as the one who teaches her the full mystery of her profession, he fulfills part of Liesl's role in relation to Eisengrim. But it is

Monica who becomes the patroness of Giles and finances his performances, as Liesl does for Eisengrim. In *A Mixture of Frailties* one is more overtly aware of what is subtly implicit in the later trilogy—that the roles are interchangeable and that Monica becomes as much an anima figure for Giles as he is an animus for her. His refusal to submit his driving and brilliant, but infantile, ego to her influence is as much as anything the cause of his death. Monica's success is that she is able to take from him the offered freedom from the tyranny of childhood and family expectations and stereotyping, but also to escape the danger of total loss of her own identity into his image of what she should be. Part of the salvation of her individuality is due to her retention of a vital connection with her Canadian roots, as Ramsay is the only one to retain a vital connection with Deptford. She goes through the process of individuation which is so important to Ramsay, David Staunton and Eisengrim and the failure of which is the real cause of Boy Staunton's despair and death.

Monica's progress towards individuation is marked by the voices in which she hears her thoughts, especially those which are judging others. At first she is surprised to find that her mental judgments of those she meets are "couched in her mother's roughest idiom" and fears that this is "a form of possession."[11] As she comes more under the influence of Giles, his voice also enters her mind, usually to undercut moments of hypocricy or pomposity on her own part. When her mother dies, Monica feels more affection and respect for her than Ramsay does for his, but an inner voice, "speaking this time not as her mother or as Giles, but in a voice which might have been her own" says, "You are free."[12] She does not lose the other voices, however, but succeeds in integrating them into her own psyche: "perhaps my substitute for thinking—orders and hints and even jokes from deep down, through the voice and personality of someone I've loved—yes, and feared?"[13]

Giles Revelstoke is the second most important character in the early trilogy as a prefiguration of the later novels. Monica's American friend, John Ripon, calls him "a Satanic genius" and as a sort of Lucifer manqué he looks towards the more successfully demonic Eisengrim of the Deptford trilogy. It is interesting that all of Revelstoke's compositions are on magical subjects. He also prefigures Boy Staunton in the series of variations on the theme of guilt produced by his "suicide." Monica at first feels that she is solely responsible for his death because she turned the gas back on when she fled his seemingly dead body. But then she is made the confidant of a string of confessions of responsibility for the suicide: from Revelstoke's mother; from Persis, his former mistress; from his friend Bun Eccles; from the music critic,

Aspenwell; and finally from Sir Benedict Domdaniel, to whom Monica confesses her own guilt. But it all comes too flatly as a rather melodramatic climax. Revelstoke's suicide is not given the numinous mystery of Boy Staunton's death, and while in both cases we finally agree that the dead man was responsible for his own fate, the death of Revelstoke does not come as the knot tying together the threads of a finely worked pattern integral to the whole novel as is the case with Staunton's death and the Deptford trilogy. The resolution of guilt in *Mixture* is too offhand. It is too easy that Domdaniel offers himself as Monica's "sin-eater" and that she "somehow" comes to terms with her guilt on the way back to Canada. Neither Liesl nor Blazon would let Ramsay off so softly in the later work. What is provocative and demanding of the reader's close attention at the end of *Fifth Business* is merely blurred and evasive at the end of *A Mixture of Frailties*.

While the two earliest novels give us only hints and fragments of what is to come in Davies' mature work, *A Mixture of Frailties* gives a fully-formed embryo. The twelve-year gap between its appearance and that of *Fifth Business* marks a period of maturing art and thought. What is too schematic, even in *Mixture*, becomes integral to character and action in *Fifth Business*. In the earlier novels, characters tend to be one-dimensional figures carrying out individual functions of plot, but a character like Ramsay can absorb Hector, Solly, Ridley, and even Monica, into a single personality with variations to spare. Likewise, description and explanation of informing ideas tend to be flatly overt in the earlier works. In following the three novels of the Salterton trilogy, we see an essayist, or journalist, becoming a novelist. For example, the prolix description of Salterton near the opening of *Tempest-Tost* is the work of an essayist doing a mood piece, including its little ironies. The similar description of Deptford near the beginning of *Fifth Business* avoids the coyness of the newspaper columnist and integrates several of the themes of the novel—religion, medicine, madness, betrayal, guilt—into three pages of economical scene-setting. Davies' governing desire to create the sense of a world of dangerous wonder behind the events of ordinary life is already apparent in the magical allusions in *Tempest-Tost*, but the transference of Prospero's island to a small estate in Salterton does not work as does the transformation of the gravel pit of Deptford into the Inferno. The greater success of the Deptford trilogy comes from its harmonious marriage of surface and symbol and of the private and public significances of the central characters as representatives of their place and time. From this harmony comes the universal significance that has given the trilogy its international success, while the balanced continuum of public

significance has given it an extraordinary appeal to the Canadian consciousness.

UNIVERSITY OF ALBERTA

NOTES

[1] *Leaven of Malice* (Toronto: Clarke Irwin, 1964 [1954]), p. 226.

[2] *Leaven,* p. 186.

[3] *Leaven,* p. 234.

[4] *Leaven,* p. 226.

[5] *A Mixture of Frailties* (Toronto: Macmillan Laurentian, 1968 [1958]),
p. 292.

[6] *Leaven,* p. 228.

[7] *One Half of Robertson Davies* (Toronto: Macmillan, 1977), p. 63. Also
in an interview on CBC Sunday Morning.

[8] *Mixture,* p. 316.

[9] *A Voice from the Attic* (Toronto: McClelland & Stewart NCL, 1972
[1960]), p. 66.

[10] C. G. Jung, *Symbols of Transformation* in *Collected Works* (Princeton:
University Press, 1970), V, 389-90.

[11] *Mixture,* p. 163.

[12] *Mixture,* p. 289.

[13] *Mixture,* p. 372.

The Folkloric Background of Robertson Davies' Deptford Trilogy

Terry Goldie

One of the great joys in the study of literature is to examine the way in which modern texts often possess resonances of a variety of earlier forms of knowledge. The analysis of these sources has caused students of writers such as Ezra Pound and T. S. Eliot to seem at times like literary detectives, who compare evidence and clues whenever they meet. Is this a mirror image of an obscure East Indian proverb? Surely that is an acronym composed from the famous Latin saying. . . .

Robertson Davies provides students of Canadian literature with similar possibilities. His Deptford trilogy drops hints of a great variety of often obscure sources, hints which critics are now beginning to pick up. Wilfred Cude, in "Miracles and Art in Fifth Business,"[1] examines the figure of St. Dunstan as presented in Eleanor Duckett's *Saint Dunstan of Canterbury*[2] and sees a very close similarity to Dunstan Ramsay in *Fifth Business*. Samuel Macey has looked at the variety of clockwork references in the trilogy and has found some very intriguing connections to eighteenth-century attitudes toward clockwork and machinery.[3] One of the earliest and most complete of these explorations is found in Patricia Monk's dissertation which explores the Jungian connections throughout Davies' work. Her analysis of *Fifth Business* in particular is highly illuminating.[4]

Jung seems to be at the centre of *Fifth Business*, and of the trilogy, but that does not mean that references to Jung can explain everything. Macey's clock analysis makes that quite clear. Jung's own sources provide suggestions of further influences on Davies. The psychologist discovered what we now call Jungian archetypes in religions, in magic, in science and pseudo-science, and in all aspects of art.

When I refer to the "Folkloric Background" I am speaking of the numerous ideas on which Davies seems to have built. Folklore is generally deemed to be the "lore of the common people" or, perhaps more clearly, that knowledge which is received through tradition and which appears to be distinct from that developed by the "elite," or educated. This definition is obviously imprecise but the overall impression should be reasonably clear. To the general public, therefore, astrology is folklore whereas astronomy is science. Even here, there are many blurred areas.

Dunstan Ramsay, and, it would seem, Robertson Davies, are quite fascinated by folklore, by tales and legends. In the study of folklore, one is often dealing with traditions which suggest a pre-rational belief. Ghost stories are one example. In *Fifth Business*, Dunstan's main interest is hagiography, or the study of saints. He does not limit himself to the perusal of dry documents of fact, but instead is often drawn more to those saints' legends which seem to have the least historical substance, such as that of St. Uncumber, the woman who grew a beard to protect her Christian chastity.

Situations like this are a constant in saints' legends. When Padre Blazon in *Fifth Business* speaks of the rather strange attributes of a number of individual saints, he is only hinting at a larger hagiographic problem. Various medieval works, most notably *The Golden Legend*,[5] describe highly unusual characters, like Simon Stylites, who became a devout hermit, living on the top of a pillar where he divided his time between prayer and various miraculous activities, such as conversing with dragons.

One of the primary studies of these strange and wonderful stories is Hippolyte Delehaye's *The Legends of the Saints*.[6] As Dunstan Ramsay notes, Delehaye was at one time the leader of the Bollandists, the scholarly body which researches saints for the Roman Catholic church, and he is probably the major hagiographer of the last two hundred years. In *Legends of the Saints*, he attempts to get rid of the St. Uncumbers. He states that there are "too many stories that are incompatible with the seriousness of true religion."[7] He rejects a number of obvious fabrications as he searches for irrefutable facts. At the same time, Delehaye cannot hide his own enjoyment of many of the most fantastic legends. He is caught in a quandary similar to that of his fictional student, Dunstan Ramsay. By the end of *Fifth Business*, that imaginary Bollandist, Padre Blazon, has persuaded Dunstan to give himself up to the inner meaning of the tales instead of the mundane facts: "That is what we call the reality of the soul; you are foolish to demand the agreement of the world as well."[8] Ramsay comes to recognize that the validity of legends is found not in their historical accuracy but in the role they play in the folklore, the guiding myths, of society. If we are to judge by his book, Delehaye was too much a servant of the Roman Catholic church to find similar freedom of mind.

The primary myth in *Fifth Business* is sainthood, and the primary saint is clearly Saint Dunstan. The book is an autobiography told by a hagiographer named Dunstan; therefore it seems not improper to view the entire story as a saint's legend. From looking at *The Golden Legend* and other sources one can see certain central patterns in the stories of saints. Gerald Pocius, in a structural analysis of saints' legends,[9] sees the pattern as (1) Call to holiness, (2) Signs of holiness, and (3) Death. Pocius' form is a bare one, as is necessitated by his attempt to approach universal application, but his study mentions other elements which, though by no means present in all, are common to many legends.

Through exploring similarities between these elements and Ramsay's life, we can see how Davies is not only following the life of St. Dunstan, as pointed out by Cude, but is also following the pattern of the saint's legend in a more general way. Like many saints, Ramsay is an unusually gifted child. Another similarity is found in his call to holiness through the intercession of an older saint, in this case, Mary Dempster, the mad fool-saint of Ramsay's home village, Deptford. Pocius notes a variety of signs of holiness, but one in this case would obviously be Dunstan's devotion to hagiography, a study pursued primarily by those in religious orders. A dominant motif in most saints' legends is the temptation by the devil, which appears in *Fifth Business* when Dunstan is tempted by Liesl. The eventual success of Liesl is not, however, the victory of evil over the saint but is instead a reconciliation of the usual dualism of good and evil. The meaning of this theological inversion will be explored below.

There are a number of other characters besides Dunstan and the elusive St. Uncumber who provide "saints' legends" of various sorts. Mary Dempster, whose unusual miracles shape Dunstan's life, is an obvious example. Surgeoner, who becomes a devout evangelist in response to Mary's selfless actions when he is in the depths of despair, is a much more minor "saint." Another figure who has great influence on Dunstan is Padre Blazon, the possessor of a number of saintly attributes. His miraculous birth is followed by a childhood in which he "seemed to be a Jesuit from the womb."[10] He is tempted by a variety of young women and then is put to a series of tests by the Jesuits because his purity is beyond their temporal understanding.

The variety of saints' legends in the novel suggests the many way in which human experience can reflect folkloric or traditional patterns. When Ramsay is examining St. Uncumber, he looks at contemporary science, folk art, pagan mythology, and even the bearded lady of the circus. All provide different hints at the meaning behind the saint.

Later, Ramsay meets Liesl, who joins Mary Dempster and Padre Blazon as a major influence in Dunstan's life. Liesl is far from a virginal Christian, but she is like St. Uncumber in being a powerful woman whose gender is at times ambiguous, whether in her masculine dress or in her sexual relationship with the beautiful Faustina. Liesl's presence in the novel gives a further dimension to the story of St. Uncumber, particularly in Liesl's association with magic and the devil, forces which are usually seen in opposition to saints.

The role of the saint's legend in the novel is complemented by an element of folklore which is clearly connected to Liesl's magic, the magus tale. The role of the magus as teacher-wizard in the Jungian cosmology is described in the second book of Davies' trilogy, *The Manticore*.[11] Another aspect is the historical and semi-historical magi. In a number of instances, saints' legends have been paired with wizard tales. The most obvious are found in *The Golden Legend*, where St. Peter meets with Simon Magus and where a number of St. Julians have to deal with Julian the Apostate. In each case the magus figure is an inversion of the saint, using evil powers in an attempt to defeat his good.

Fifth Business presents similar figures, although the pattern is not such a simple triumph of good over evil. As Jung would suggest, the dark knowledge of the magus proves just as essential as the light of the saint. At the most obvious level, this is reflected by Dunstan as developing saint and Magnus Eisengrim as the developing magus. Both the name Magnus and his earlier title of Faustus LeGrand have connections to legendary magi. The pattern of Magnus' life is certainly a legendary one: birth in strange circumstances; demonstration of great skill at an early age; exile in youth; a series of trials, including overcoming two "monsters," Willard and Liesl, before he achieves his great power.[12]

As with the saints, the magus references occur on a number of different levels. In his article in this volume, Macey has noted a very subtle comment in that one of the Faust writers, Christopher Marlowe, was killed in Deptford on Thames, the ancestor of the Canadian town which gives birth to Dunstan and Magnus. Just as there are other saints, so there are other magi. Liesl, particularly in her role as the voice of the Brazen Head, is very much a wizard figure. Just as Blazon is one part saint, so is he one part magus; his last name and his cunning actions in causing the nursing sisters to read heretical literature suggest some connection with a darker power. Even that minor vision of shadowy sensuality, Faustina, seems to have some role to play here, if only as a quite unconscious representative of the devil.

The mention of the Brazen Head should send us on another folkloric expedition. The legendary magi, like Simon Magus, have been followed by those who have been to at least some extent historically documented, like the original Faust. According to E. M. Butler, in *The Myth of the Magus*, a

25

number of such figures in the Renaissance were drawn to experiments with the Brazen Head, an oracular machine originally associated with Roger Bacon.[13] One student of the occult who followed Bacon was John Dee, with his alchemist associate, Edward Kelly. Their connection to the Brazen Head in Davies' novel may seem no more than an interesting footnote but there is more to this relationship. Dee was convinced that Kelly had found the essence of alchemical knowledge in an old manuscript. This manuscript is *The Book of Saint Dunstan.*

If one accepts the above argument that the novel is a form of saint's legend, it does not seem absurd to subtitle *Fifth Business,* "the Book of Saint Dunstan." It is unclear exactly what *The Book of Saint Dunstan* was. William Stubbs, in *Memorials of Saint Dunstan,*[14] notes a number of alchemical works which were attributed to Saint Dunstan, for no apparent reason other than Dunstan's great prestige and his traditional association with metal craft. A. E. Waite[15] suggests that a series of verses left by Kelly might be in fact his metrical translation of the book. A carefully described chemical experiment is preceded by a philosophical introduction, the essence of which seems quite similar to statements by other alchemists. The verses maintain that the successful alchemical process must bring together the purest Mercury and Sulfur, and join them like the purest man and wife:

> Now what is meant by man and wife is this,
> Agent and patient, yet not two but one,
> Even as was Eva Adam's wife I wisse,
> Flesh of his flesh and bone of his bone—
> Such is the unionhood of our precious Stone;
> As Adam slept until his wife was made,
> Even so our Stone; there can no more be said.[16]

The wife herself is a resolution of all possible opposites: "Therefore the true wife which I doe mean / Of all these contraries is the meane betweene."[17]

The goal of the process is the Philosopher's Stone, the catalyst to produce gold from base metal. To attain this power, the Stone must include all possible agents, no matter what they might be. This is why the "wife" must be the resolution of opposites. In fact, Kelly's process suggests that what appears to be the antithesis to the desired end is the proper direction, as in the following: "But if through blackness thou to whiteness march / Then it will be both white and soft as starch."[18]

This is no easy paradox but as Jung himself said, "Only the paradox comes anywhere near to comprehending the fulness of life."[19] The association of opposites is described quite clearly through the various magi and saints in

Fifth Business. After Dunstan's encounter with the devil in the form of Liesl, Padre Blazon points out:

> The Devil knows corners of us all of which Christ Himself is ignorant. Indeed, I am sure Christ learned a great deal that was salutary about Himself when He met the Devil in the wilderness. Of course, that was a meeting of brothers; people forget too readily that Satan is Christ's elder brother and has certain advantages in argument that pertain to a senior. On the whole, we treat the Devil shamefully, and the worse we treat Him the more He laughs at us. . . . You met the Devil as an equal, not cringing or frightened or begging for a trashy favour. That is the heroic life, Ramezay. You are fit to be the Devil's friend, without any fear of losing yourself to Him!"[20]

Throughout the trilogy, Davies asserts the need to achieve a proper balance between various polarities, such as masculine and feminine, reason and emotion, light and dark, saint and magus, and good and evil. In *The Manticore*, Davies shows Jung's belief in this balance of opposites as a therapist uses dream analysis to help Davy Staunton to raise his unconscious, his feelings, his dreams, to meet the overwhelming power of his conscious, his intellect, his reason. *Fifth Business* presents his father, Boy Staunton, as a wealthy industrialist, for whom all is conscious, all reason. Mary Dempster, the fool-saint, lives in a dream world, apparently unconscious of what we would call reality. Through Blazon and Liesl, Ramsay seems to become "of all these contraries, the meane betweene."

In *Psychology and Alchemy*, Jung examines this state represented in the alchemic coniunctio, the joining of man and woman, of sun and moon, of light and dark:

> The point is that alchemy is rather like an undercurrent to the Christianity that ruled on the surface. It is to this surface as the dream is to consciousness, and just as the dream compensates the conflicts of the conscious mind, so alchemy endeavours to fill in the gaps left open by the Christian tension of opposites.[21]

This alchemic balance, found in the Philosopher's Stone, is not only the means of producing gold from dross. In *Alchemy*, E. J. Holmyard points out that a mystical dimension is also implied: "The Stone was also sometimes known as the Elixir or Tincture, and was credited not only with the power of transmutation but with that of prolonging human life indefinitely."[22] It is like the knowledge which Ramsay achieves in *Fifth Business*, which enables him to get progressively closer to a full understanding of himself. Certain aspects of this vision take him "beyond death," both when lost on the battlefield and when stricken with a heart attack in the theatre.

27

Like Ramsay's image of Mary Dempster on the battlefield, the Stone was the means to a higher state. It performed a similar function with both metal and man. It was never the goal but the means to the ultimate goal of perfection. Because perfect, this state was maintained to be beyond clear representation and beyond simple comprehension, as in Jung's earlier statement about the paradox. This tendency to obscurity is evident in the following quotation from Zosimos, an Egyptian alchemist: "In speaking of the Philosopher's Stone, receive this Stone which is not a Stone, a precious thing which has no value, a thing of many shapes, this unknown which is known of all."[23]

John Dee recalled having seen "the famous 'angelical stone'; a thing 'most bright, most clere and glorious, of the bigness of an egg.' "[24] Above, the Stone is compared to the statue of Mary in *Fifth Business*, in that both provide a visionary power which apparently overcomes mortality. A different and perhaps more fruitful link might be to Ramsay's little paperweight, "an ordinary piece of pinkish granite about the size of a small egg."[25] It seems ordinary but it takes on extraordinary importance.

Fifth Business begins when Boy Staunton throws the stone, hidden in a snowball. This action causes Mary Dempster's madness, the birth of the boy who will be Magnus Eisengrim, and Dunstan Ramsay's devotion to Mary Dempster, which leads to his study of saints. At the end of *Fifth Business*, Boy Staunton has died with the stone in his mouth. In Magnus's magic performance, Liesl cryptically refers to "the keeper of the stone" as one of the causes of Boy's death. This precipitates Ramsay's heart attack, as he recognizes himself as the one who held the stone as a reminder of his own and Boy's guilt.

The stone is therefore central to both opening and conclusion of *Fifth Business*. The "keeper of the stone" speech comes in response to Davy Staunton's question about his father and the answer sends him to Switzerland, to pursue the analysis which is recorded in *The Manticore*. Davy is now the "keeper of the stone," which he took from his father's body. At the end of this novel, Ramsay throws away the stone, an action which seems to symbolize Davy overcoming his slavery to his father's memory.

The final work of the trilogy, *World of Wonders*, does not seem to have a similar obsession, but the last few pages once more return to Boy's death and the stone. Magnus told Boy to "swallow that stone" and face his evil past. Since Boy had always avoided confronting his inner self, this final meeting could end only in his death. Ramsay tells Liesl his present impressions of the stone and the death: "Magnus thinks I kept the stone for spite, and I suppose there was something of that in it. But I also kept it to be a continual reminder of the consequences that can follow a single action."[26]

That single action in one way or another causes the rest of the trilogy. The stone is much more than just a "reminder." It has a resemblance to Ramsay's father's stone, a granite paperweight which represents his harsh Presbyterian past. A folklorist might call it a representative aspect of material culture, a symbol of the people whose lives have developed in association with it. Before Ramsay throws away his stone, he speaks to Davy of its age: "something like a thousand million years old. Where has it been, before there were any men to throw it, and where will it be when you and I are not even a pinch of dust? . . . None of us counts for much in the long, voiceless inert history of the stone."[27]

Throughout the trilogy, we are dealing with saints and magi, the agents of God and the agents of a darker power, perhaps the devil. In *Fifth Business*, Ramsay explores the folk representations of Christianity in statuary and other forms. Is it too extreme to see the stone as the opposite, the representation of the devil? It spawns a series of apparently evil actions, causing madness, death and years of psychological torture for many. And yet, as Magnus points out at the end of *World of Wonders*, there is a way in which the stone helped him to achieve great knowledge. The same could be said, in very different ways, of Ramsay, of Davy Staunton, and even of Boy, although this knowledge led to his death.

Once again we should look back to Jung and the religious vision in alchemy. He shows how many alchemical philosophers saw the Philosopher's Stone, this means to eternal life, as having some of the attributes of Christ. Is it possible that this stone of St. Dunstan in *Fifth Business*, the stone of Dunstan Ramsay, is at once the agent of good and evil?

Ramsay's stone is in one way very different from the Philosopher's Stone. It is not something which is sought but something which each character devotes his life to escaping. Like the Philosopher's Stone, however, it seems a representation of diabolic power but with decisive positive applications. Like Kelly's *The Book of Saint Dunstan*, it brings the opposites together. The stone is the reconciliation of the opposite parts of folklore which we meet in the saints' legends and magus tales. In *Fifth Business*, Dunstan Ramsay learns how to live with both God and the Devil, an understanding which the alchemist-saint of Kelly's book would have been forced to achieve.

Again like the Philosopher's Stone, Ramsay's stone is not the final goal but a means to that goal. It is the catalyst for the transmutation of a number of lives. Ramsay and the other characters must explore the paths of the saint and of the magus to reach the "fulness of life" of which Jung wrote. The

29

paradoxical stone helps each to see the meaning of his own process of individuation, of coming to terms with himself. As Jung states, "The self is a union of opposites *par excellence*."[28]

In a sophisticated trilogy of fiction, Davies follows an exploratory route which seems very much in a Jungian pattern. The path leads through legends of saints and magi as Ramsay tries to reconcile the dark and the light sides of the human personality. With him is the everpresent stone, which acts as a complement to his memory of Mary Dempster as he researches both the most holy and most satanic of mysteries. Through all this there are hints of the alchemic process, of *The Book of Saint Dunstan* and the Philosopher's Stone, of the medieval attempts to join the disparate parts of the universe to reach a perfect whole.

Jung himself would admit, however, that this "Jungian pattern" is only an effort to explain through contemporary educated processes what the "folk" have long "understood." Like Jung, the scholarly Ramsay must spend a long life until he can comprehend and accept what the man of the middle ages and the renaissance knew implicitly through what we might call "superstitions." The series of quotation marks employed in this last paragraph suggests the distance between our usual understanding of these words and concepts and the understanding which Ramsay finally reaches. Davies might say that many of the dualisms in the universe must be reassessed, including even "fact and fiction." As Padre Blazon says to Ramsay, "You must find your answer in psychological truth, not objective truth. . . ."[29] Perhaps this is the ultimate "fact" in the folkloric fiction of the Deptford trilogy.

MEMORIAL UNIVERSITY OF NEWFOUNDLAND

NOTES

[1] Wilfred Cude, "Miracle and Art in *Fifth Business*," *Journal of Canadian Studies*, 9 (November 1974), 3-16.

[2] Eleanor Shipley Duckett, *Saint Dunstan of Canterbury* (London: Collins, 1955).

[3] See "Time, Clockwork, and the Devil in Robertson Davies' Deptford Trilogy" in this volume.

[4] Patricia Monk, "The Smaller Infinity: The Jungian Self in the Novels of Robertson Davies." Ph.D. dissertation, Queen's University, 1974.

[5] Jacobus de Voragine, *The Golden Legend*, a modern translation by Granger Ryan and Helmut Ripperberger (New York: Arno Press, 1969, reprint 1941 ed.).

[6] Hippolyte Delehaye, *Legends of the Saints* (New York: Fordham University Press, 1962).

[7] *Ibid.*, p. xv.

[8] Robertson Davies, *Fifth Business* (New York: Signet, 1971), p. 156.

[9] Gerald L. Pocius, "The Life of the Saint: A Structural Analysis of *The Golden Legend.*" Unpublished manuscript. Memorial University of Newfoundland Folklore and Language Archive.

[10] Davies, *Fifth Business*, p. 157.

[11] Robertson Davies, *The Manticore* (New York: Curtis, 1972), p. 238.

[12] This could be compared to the various heroic patterns explored in Lord Raglan's *The Hero: A Study in Tradition, Myth, and Drama* (London: Methuen, 1936) or Jan de Vries' *Heroic Song and Heroic Legend*, trans. B. J. Timmer (London: Oxford University Press, 1963).

[13] E. M. Butler, *The Myth of the Magus* (Cambridge: Cambridge University Press, 1948). The Brazen Head dominates Robert Greene's play *Friar Bacon and Friar Bungay* (*c.* 1590).

[14] William Stubbs, *Memorials of Saint Dunstan* (Wiesbaden, Germany: Kraus Reprint, 1965, reprint 1875 London ed.).

[15] A. E. Waite, *The Alchemical Writings of Edward Kelly* (London: Stuart and Watkins, 1970), p. xliii.

[16] *Ibid.*, p. xliv.

[17] *Ibid.*, p. xlvii.

[18] *Ibid.*, p. li.

[19] Carl Gustav Jung, *Psychology and Alchemy*, translated R. F. C. Hull (Princeton, New Jersey: Princeton University Press, 1977), p. 19.

[20] Davies, *Fifth Business*, pp. 222-23.

[21] Jung, *Psychology and Alchemy*, p. 23.

[22] E. J. Holmyard, *Alchemy* (Harmondsworth, Middlesex, England: Penguin, 1968), p. 15.

[23] Ronald Pearsall, *The Alchemists* (London: Weidenfield and Nicolson, 1976), pp. 48-49.

[24] E. M. Butler, quoting from the manuscript of John Dee's "Spiritual Diary" [as recorded in Charlotte Fell-Smith, *John Dee* (London: Constable, 1909), p. 86], *The Myth of the Magus*, p. 165.

[25] Davies, *Fifth Business*, p. 224.

[26] Robertson Davies, *World of Wonders* (Toronto: Macmillan, 1975), p. 357.

[27] Davies, *The Manticore*, pp. 300-01.

[28] Jung, *Psychology and Alchemy*, p. 19.

[29] Davies, *Fifth Business*, p. 160.

Time, Clockwork, and the Devil in Robertson Davies' Deptford Trilogy

Samuel L. Macey

I. INTRODUCTION

Robertson Davies' Deptford trilogy is much concerned with the place of the Devil in the life of modern man. The ambivalence of the author towards his characters lends a rich complexity to his works, but an examination of the idiom in which he writes—the idiom that relates the modern Western technological Devil to time and clockwork—will help us towards an understanding of the novels.

All but one of the major characters in the trilogy come from the small Canadian town of Deptford on the River Thames. As with the Faust of Marlowe (an author himself mysteriously killed in Deptford upon Thames), the good angels from above and the bad angels from below compete for their souls.[1] The Devil with whom we are here concerned is, however, essentially modern and puritan.

Before the age of Western technology, Marlowe's Faust—as in the *Volksbuch* on which his story is based—sells himself to the Devil for twenty-four years of pleasures upon earth. When the time is up at the striking of the eleventh hour (after the horologically symbolic twice times twelve years), Marlowe's Faust says: "The starres moove stil, time runs, the clocke will strike . . ." and Faustus must be damned (V. ii. 141-142). Marlowe's clock, though then an innovation for the stage, was still an innocent mechanism for denoting time. With the Romantic poets, however, clocks and clockworks begin to take on quite different connotations.

The great revolution in clockwork, the British horological revolution, came between 1660 and 1760, and did far more to herald the industrial revolution than is generally recognized. During the horological revolution, one did not, of course, relate clocks and clockwork to the Devil. On the contrary, that was the period of ascendancy for the Watchmaker God, the period when Tompion and Graham, the mechanic fathers of horology, were buried in

Westminster Abbey, and when Samuel Clarke (on behalf of Newton) argued with Leibniz only whether God needed to rewind his watch of the universe. But old gods—like Saturn, himself the god of time—have a way of becoming devils; with the Romantic poets, clocks and clockworks began to take on the sinister connotations that they have today. Baudelaire talks of "Horloge! dieu sinistre";[2] Tennyson, unlike Milton, tells us that "There is a clock in Pandemonium";[3] Hoffmann's automaton, Olympia, is as sinister as her clockmaker "father"; Poe writes spine-chilling stories like "Predicament" and "The Pit and the Pendulum"; and, ultimately, Samuel Butler's *Erewhon* describes a pastoral Utopia where it is considered that the only safe place for the watch is in a museum.

The pejorative connotations of clockwork are still with us: a fictional James Agate, for example—when writing of Tresize's *Master of Ballantrae* in *World of Wonders*—"condemned the play, which he likened to clockwork."[4] But the clockwork idiom has also entered into our language in ways that we now hardly notice: in *The Manticore*, Johanna von Haller argues that early toilet training "is not the mainspring of life";[5] in *World of Wonders*, Magnus Eisengrim—alias Faustus Legrand, alias Paul Dempster—argues that "a theatrical production is a mechanism of exquisitely calculated details" (280).

Clockwork has done more than enter the idiom of our language; it has enslaved all of us who work with a watch strapped to our wrists. This is the important change wrought by modern WASP technology with its seventeenth-century roots in the clockwork dog of the Cartesian mechanistic philosophy, the empirical and utilitarian science of Francis Bacon, and the related horological revolution.

The horological revolution produced the first mechanical timepieces sufficiently accurate for the domestic use of modern man. It also made a significant contribution to batch production and the subdivision of labour in industry, thereby regulating urban work by time other than sunrise and sunset. In the nineteenth century, railways—with their time zones, telegraphs, and railway watches—added a further dimension to the industrial revolution and to man's servitude to time.

It is from Deptford, a small Canadian railway town, that the main characters in this story set out. (The only apparent exception is Liesl, Calvinist heir to a Swiss horological empire.) The narrator in *Fifth Business* is Dunstan Ramsay, a Deptford boy who became a writer of books on saints, a holder of the Victoria Cross, and a long-time eccentric schoolmaster in history. At the age of just over three score and ten years, he writes *Fifth Business* in the form of a confessional "memoir" addressed to his "Headmaster,"[6] or perhaps to his God. His writings show that the Scots Presbyterian or Calvinist Dunstan is very much a slave to time. Nothing could be more precise than his opening paragraph: "My lifelong involvement with Mrs. Dempster began at 5:58 o'clock p.m. on the 27th of December, 1908, at which time I was ten years and seven months old." At that time—although the presence of the stone is not revealed until much later—Dunstan's contemporary, Boy Staunton, threw at him a snowball containing a pink granite stone.

Let us remind ourselves briefly of some of the events in the Deptford trilogy which ensue from that action. By avoiding the snowball, Dunstan allowed it to hit Mary Dempster, the wife of the Baptist minister. On the following day, Mary was delivered of a three-pound baby, Paul Dempster, who arrived eighty days before he was due. Mary became insane, and Dunstan, who thought of her as a saint and nurtured his guilt, kept the stone secretly for over fifty years.

At the end of *Fifth Business*, Boy Staunton, who is now seventy, is about to become the Lieutenant-Governor of Ontario. After speaking with Magnus Eisengrim for the first time, he commits suicide with the stone in his mouth. At the end of *The Manticore*, David Staunton, scion of a house that controls some eighty percent of Canada's sugar trade, lets Dunstan throw away the stone. *The Manticore* is virtually a journal of his life written for the Jungian psychiatrist Johanna von Haller. She tries to inject more feeling into the totally cerebral and dangerously alcoholic David whose life has been lived in the shadow of Boy Staunton, epitome of the North-American dream of boundless energy, sexual athleticism, and the acquisition of great wealth. At the end of *The Manticore*, David feels that he must choose between Liesl Vitzlipützli—a brilliant mechanic and the heiress to a horological fortune who has taken the name of one of the demons in a pre-Goethian version of *Faust* (*Wonders*, 332)—and Johanna—whose name means "God is gracious." At the end of *World of Wonders*, however—in which Dunstan relates the story of Magnus Eisengrim—there is much to suggest that a choice between black and white does not really have to be made.

2. THE SERVITUDE TO TIME

Let us return to the particularly precise form of time that controls both Dunstan and Deptford. Dunstan tells us that five years after the birth of her son, Mary Dempster's wanderings, which are related to her insanity, come to an end just before ten o'clock on the night of Friday 24th of October, 1913. At that time, she goes to the pit, a "Protestant Hell" or "Gehenna" beside Deptford, and sacrifices herself to a tramp in a most un-Protestant manner merely because "he wanted it so badly" (*Fifth*, 41-44). Deptford itself is later called "that hole."

When Dunstan returns after leaving a leg behind in the Europe of World War I, there is typical precision in the way that Deptford times the welcoming celebration for the hero, and the returning soldiers each receive railway watches as gifts that are warranted to be accurate (*Fifth*, 85-89). Deptford's servitude to the Satanic qualities of Time is of course symbolic of Western civilization. Thoreau had said of the railways and their clocks: "One well conducted institution regulates a whole country,"[7] and Melville's Ahab had said of the men under his Satanic control: "My one cogged circle fits into their various wheels, and they revolve."[8]

Timekeeping is in the warp and woof of Deptford. Not only does Dunstan briefly become a timekeeper on roadwork, as Paul's father had become a timekeeper in the sawmill after the family's disgrace (*Fifth*, 99, 46), but the two objects that represent his now dead parents are his father's desk with the stone paperweight, and his mother's clock. While Dunstan had been away, the letters of the physically beautiful Leola came "like clockwork" every second Sunday, and like clockwork they were without feeling. Instead of marrying Dunstan, Leola (whose name means "lioness") later became the rejected wife of Boy Staunton. She was the mother of David, the Manticore with a lion's body, a man's head, and a sting in his tail (*Manticore*, 175).

Though Dunstan's visits to Mary Dempster are, as we shall see, the result of an attraction of opposites, he both carefully documents and carefully times them (*Fifth*, 143, 162). There is a comparable irony in the way that Canadians are brought—through the touring theatrical company of Sir John Tresize—those elements of romance which will provide "a warm, safe place where Time hardly moves at all." Though it certainly provides romance, the whole English company moves to Vancouver and back under the advance management of Morton W. Penfold who delights in "a real railway watch— one of those gigantic nickel-plated turnips that kept very accurate time" (*Wonders*, 252, 265).

Dunstan's precision regarding time carries over quite naturally into precision regarding money. By the time that he negotiates the royalties for ghost-writing Eisengrim's "autobiography," we can sympathize with that magician's remark about the "grasping Ramsay blood" of the Calvinist Scot (*Fifth*, 188). After World War I, Dunstan and Boy both start with $5,000 each. Dunstan carefully increased this sum to $8,000, while Boy achieved a "plum" ($100,000) by shrewd financial methods. Such methods will eventually earn more than one hundred million dollars for Boy, who becomes Canada's Minister of Food during World War II (*Fifth*, 107, 113).

Attracted by money and by the vicarious link that it brings him with the mystery of wealth, Dunstan retains his connection with Boy Staunton, and through his help not only continues to accumulate a limited fortune but also avoids the painful stock market crash in 1929 (*Fifth*, 1, 127-128).

Perhaps even more symptomatic of his precision with money are Dunstan Ramsay's by now typical reactions to sharing the cost of staying at the Savoy Hotel in the latter part of *World of Wonders* (160, *et passim*). In fact, the older Dunstan first began to think better of Eisengrim, the world's leading magician, when he returned with interest the money that he had stolen from him under the alias of Faustus Legrand. As Dunstan put it, "I appreciate scrupulosity in money matters" (*Fifth*, 184-185). But we suspect that Eisengrim may not normally be as scrupulous in matters of finance. In fact when Dunstan eventually persuades him to pay part of the support for his insane mother, Liesl suggests a banker's order because "she knew that if he had to send . . . cheques he would forget very soon" (*Fifth*, 205).

Both Eisengrim and his mother Mary are untypical of Deptford in their relationship with time. (They are also untypical insofar as their feelings tend to dominate their thinking.) Dunstan tells us that Mary "had no sense of time," and regarded him "as the only constant factor in her life" (*Fifth*, 206).

Though others see Mary as a "Fool Saint" (*Fifth Business*, Part III), she seems to provide Dunstan with a complementary ideal unrelated to mercenary or temporal values. His lifelong study of saints derives from what he considers to be her three miracles. We have already referred to the first miracle, the saving of the tramp, Surgeoner, by offering him true but un-Protestant *caritas*, or love, in the "Protestant Hell" beside Deptford (*Fifth*, 44, 117, 120-122; *Manticore*, 160). The second miracle involves her bringing back of Dunstan's elder brother Willie from the dead. Writing of the experience, Dunstan says, "The passing of time that afternoon was all awry." That Dunstan should have called in Mary, the town's outcast, exasperates his mother, and the boy's enlistment is precipitated by forcing a choice between his mother's rectitude and his love for Mary (*Fifth*, 55-58). Again at Passchendaele—where the vision of Mary Dempster's face on the Madonna provides the third miracle that saves him from death and gains him a "posthumous" Victoria Cross—Dunstan is untypically incapable of remembering the exact day (*Fifth*, 66, 70, 223-224, also 144-146, 218-219). Mary's transcendence of Deptford's enslavement to time extends beyond the effect that she has on Dunstan. When Dunstan, though forbidden to visit her, says farewell to Mary before leaving for the Front, she speaks as if he had "visited her as often as usual." And when Dunstan, years later, bids her good-bye on her deathbed, she says, "Are you Dunstable Ramsay.... I thought he was a boy" (*Fifth*, 59, 217)?

This lack of a sense of time in Deptford's outsider, Mary, is also reflected in her son, the outsider Paul. In marked contrast to Dunstan, Eisengrim's account of his life in *World of Wonders* includes such typical remarks as: "I was seventeen or eighteen ... I had long forgotten my birthday"; "it must have been fourteen years" since I met Dunstan; "I must have been twenty-two"; or "It ... was from a novel, by somebody-or-other.... I make no pretence of being an exact historian" (137, 144, 176, 121).

Unlike Dunstan—who finds his complementary qualities in the sainthood of Paul's mother Mary, the "little Madonna" of "the Immaculate Conception" (*Fifth*, 70-71)—Eisengrim finds his complementary qualities as a mechanic and clockmaker of almost magical virtuosity. He tells us in *World of Wonders* that he had become a "reanimator of clocks" because he had gained "a contempt for time ... sitting inside Abdullah [the card-playing "automaton" of Wanless's World of Wonders], when time had no significance" (304-305). Later, Eisengrim is called in to repair the broken automata of Herr Direktor Jeremias Naegeli at Sorgenfrei. The old man, descendant of a great Swiss horological empire, is particularly impressed by Eisengrim's insistence that he "mustn't be pressed for time." Naegli accepted the fact that Eisengrim was "never [to be] harried ... about time," and also that he was not to be bothered by the industrialist's "demand for accurate figures" (*Wonders*, 311-312).

Precisely because Eisengrim is generally vague about time, one notes two dates (at the beginning and end of *World of Wonders*) that, atypically, he remembers all too well. The first date is "August 30, 1918. That was the day I descended into hell [or Willard's Abdullah] and did not rise again for seven years"; the second date is November 3, 1968, the night when the magician Eisengrim allowed Boy Staunton to go to his death with the stone in his mouth, the same stone that had made Paul Dempster an outcast sixty years earlier (15, 346).

3. EISENGRIM, THE "MAGICIAN" CLOCKMAKER

Though Paul Dempster never returned to Deptford—except to spit briefly and anonymously at the town when travelling across Canada with Sir John Tresize's touring company—his relationship with watches and mechanics, as well as with the theatre, is rooted in that town. At Sorgenfrei, he explains the qualities that go into the making of a magician even greater than Robert-Houdin (Jean Eugène Robert, 1805-71), the role he plays in a film for the

37

BBC. The reader may remember that the first great conjuring feat which Eisengrim's boyhood teacher, Dunstan, studied in Deptford, came ironically enough from Robert-Houdin's book *The Secrets of Stage Conjuring*. This involved the typical recovery of a shah's jewelled watch that had apparently been smashed to pieces.

In the eyes of the egoistic Eisengrim, Robert-Houdin had been a bourgeois, "a deserving young watch- and clock-maker" whose "mechanical devices" miss Eisengrim's "controlled sympathy" with the audience (*Wonders*, 59, 3-5). But Eisengrim's egoism is justified by his student Liesl: "Any great craft tends at last towards the condition of a philosophy, and I was moving through clockwork to the Magian World View." The Spenglerian Magian World View is "something only the great scientists have . . . the lesser ones are merely clockmakers of a larger growth, just as many of our humanist scholars are just cud-chewers or system grinders" (*Wonders*, 323-324; *Fifth*, 192-193).

But even a great mechanic must begin somewhere, and Eisengrim—who had taken intuitively to the card tricks and money palming taught to him by the literary but ham-handed Dunstan (*Fifth*, 36-38)—left Deptford at the age of ten and joined Wanless's World of Wonders. There he became both willingly and unwillingly the sex slave of the Mephistophelian dope addict Willard the Wizard, and spent seven years as the human gaff inside the card-playing "automaton" Abdullah.[9]

Like the Chess Player in Poe's story of "Maelzel's Chess Player," Abdullah was only a make-believe automaton, but it did have sham mechanisms that Eisengrim learned how to keep in repair. A Dutchman named Henry—who had been trained as a clock- and watch-maker in boyhood—taught him about clockwork. He gave Eisengrim a watch—a big, old-fashioned silver turnip—which he took to pieces again and again. Then one day, when opportunity served, he stole a wristwatch for the same purpose and he also "sometimes haunted watch-repair shops." In this way, Eisengrim's "seven years as the mechanism of Abdullah" served to make him a "deft mechanic," and taught him much both about clockwork and about the people whom he could observe without being seen. As Eisengrim puts it, "People love to frighten themselves"; they "cannot resist automata." We shall have more to say about the Devil that automata in general and Abdullah in particular had come to represent. We may note, however, that Abdullah's name means "the servant of God." In a trilogy with strong Manichaean overtones, such a name is rather more apposite for the mechanical hell in which Eisengrim served than Robertson Davies would seem to allow (*Wonders*, 52-55, 148, 64, 95, 112-113, 123).

After the death of Willard the Wizard (his father in magic, whom he had taken to Europe), Eisengrim went to England. When he was a penniless busker in London, he was given the chance to play as the anonymous double to Sir John Tresize and offered his old silver watch as a pledge for the advance of thirty shillings in wages. His clothes at that time were so poor that he was warned away from the watch-and-clock exhibit at the Victoria and Albert Museum, but his mechanical skill helped him to double also as the assistant stage manager to the company. Almost a decade later (when Eisengrim had buried Sir John, his father in stagecraft and dramatic romance), his uncanny knack with clocks was to help him again. By this time, he had been accepted as a repairer of fine old clocks at the Victoria and Albert Museum, because he had that rare "sympathy that isn't directly hitched to mechanical knowledge" (*Wonders*, 304-306), but he left for Switzerland just before World War II.

With a letter of recommendation from the curator of the Victoria and Albert, Eisengrim was able to obtain a job at the Musée d'Art et d'Histoire in Geneva. This led via the fortuitous repair of a valuable mechanical toy to his job with Herr Direktor Jeremias Naegeli at Sorgenfrei. Naegeli "owned the most extraordinary collection of mechanical toys that anyone has ever seen," and which "is now in one of the museums in Zürich" (*Wonders*, 310). The collection of some 150 automata dated back to between 1790 and the 1830's and '40s. It had been almost completely destroyed by Naegeli's hideous granddaughter and heiress, Liesl (*Wonders*, 314).

In a manner analogous to the increasing accuracy of watches, automata acquired in the eighteenth century a verisimilitude probably far greater and certainly more readily authenticated than such earlier and probably mythic automata as the Brazen Head of Friar Bacon, which plays such an important role in the trilogy. The most famous eighteenth-century automata were Vaucanson's two musicians and his duck that was credited with "eating, drinking, mascerating the food and voiding excrements." Vaucanson made a fortune exhibiting these between 1737 and 1743.[10] In 1774, the Jaquet-Droz, father and son, founded a firm in London. Bedini describes the Writer, the Artist, and the Young Girl playing a Clavichord, their most famous life-sized clockwork androids, which have survived. Their fourth piece, the Grotto, appears to have been broken up under the accusation of witchcraft when it went to Spain.[11]

Such versatile modern clockwork androids, which lent credence to the age-old power dream that man might imitate or even eliminate the function of God, seem to have fascinated and yet horrified the Romantic poets. The dream in non-mechanical terms becomes a Frankenstein; in mechanical terms it becomes the beautiful yet clockwork Olympia of E. T. A. Hoffmann's *Tales*. Indeed it is precisely because Liesl—who looked like Kundry the evil enchantress in *Parsifal*—had seen the *Tales of Hoffmann* that she destroyed her father's priceless collection (*Wonders*, 320). The irony is that, once tamed by Eisengrim, she, too, achieved the Magian World View by helping him to reanimate the androids. In this way she earned the right to become the owner of a Sorgenfrei worthy of its name.

But in the trilogy the fear of becoming an automaton is not limited to Liesl. Though Boy Staunton appears to have attained the Canadian Protestant dream, he never achieved that balance in life typical of those who live in Sorgenfrei, a balance which by the end of *The Manticore* seems even to be within the reach of his son David. At the end of *World of Wonders* it seems possible that Boy Staunton abdicates from life because he fears that the ceremonial element in the duties of a Lieutenant-Governor would make him "no more than the animation of that uniform" (*Wonders*, 351). Like Paul Dempster, whom his action had condemned to seven years in the hell of Abdullah many years earlier, he sees himself as the human gaff for an "automaton."

Eisengrim's *Brazen Head of Friar Bacon* is, of course, another important gaffed "automaton"—a good thought-reading act "that would have done credit to the oracle at Delphi"—which plays an important role in all three novels. It speaks at the end of *Fifth Business* when David Staunton demands of it in the Royal Alexandra Theatre at Toronto: "Who killed Boy Staunton?" (189-191, 237-238). The enigmatic reply of the Brazen Head leads on first to *The Manticore*, where David tries to make sense of his life as the Absalom to his father, and, secondly, to *World of Wonders*, because Eisengrim's fears and Dunstan's heart attack hasten their departure with Leisl for the geriatric pleasures of Sorgenfrei (*Manticore*, 4, 59-61; *Wonders*, 338ff.).

4.   SORGENFREI: COMING TO TERMS WITH THE DIABOLISM
OF TIME

When Dunstan tells us, "I should be surprised if the Devil didn't invent Time, with all the subtle terrors that Time comprises" (*Wonders*, 60), he is doing more than transferring the child-eating and time-denoting qualities from Saturn-Cronus to Satan, the antagonist of God. The modern Satan terminates life with the mechanical precision of the clock in Marlowe's *Faust*, and also chains man to a technological clockwork rigidity unknown to the gods of old.

Much of the modern Satanic terminology naturally remains the same: Deptford's gravel pit is a "Gehenna," the theatre is the "Devil's domain," Dunstan is a "snake in the grass," Eisengrim's "blasphemous soul panted after" Willard the Wizard with his Mephistophelian smile, Netty (David's nurse) is the "Demon Queen," David is a "saturnine lawyer-wizard," Leisl has her nose twisted by Ramsay in his role as Saint Dunstan, and at the end of *The Manticore* she prays to the ancient bear deities "like a demon in the cave." Even Boy Staunton, outwardly the least Satanic of the protagonists, lives "deep in some egotistical hell of his own."

A part of Willard and his experience in the automaton Abdullah remains in Eisengrim and is manifested by his "Mephistophelian smile." Liesl tells us that Calvinists like Dunstan and Eisengrim must fight with dragons which become a part of them and naturally something of the dragon shows. As has been demonstrated earlier in this paper, the dragon in modern society can most readily be understood in terms of modern man's enslavement to Time and its mechanical symbol of clockwork. We can, however, no longer smash our clockwork or hive it off in museums. If we are to seek a Manichaean co-existence between evil and good, black and white, night and day—as suggested by the juxtaposition of Liesl and Johanna on the last page of *The Manticore* and of the Devil and God on the last page of *World of Wonders* —we must understand evil in terms of today's technological idiom.

Let us consider how David Staunton as well as the three regular inhabitants of Sorgenfrei come to terms with the diabolism of Time. David may say of Sorgenfrei that it is "positively the damnedest house I have ever entered," but it is also the house in which each must play the game of chess, like the game of life, with both the black and the white pieces on the five levels of a multiple chess-board (*Manticore*, 275-276, 291). The house itself is a paradox: a piece of Gothic romance where time hardly moves at all (*Wonders*, 252), but yet a house full of clockwork automata and dominated by a master clock that combines modern time with an automated Morality Play featuring the older agricultural measures of time, "the figures of Day and Night, the Seasons, two heads of Time . . . " (*Manticore*, 283).

For David, the two heads of Time—that Janus-figure which at the winter solstice looks back and forwards—has long been the problem with which he must come to terms. This is the period when Christ would have been born in myth if he had not been born in fact. It is also the period when Boy Staunton causes the premature birth of Paul, when Leola tries to commit suicide, when David is involved with Judith Wolff in a Christmas play, when David has the only night of sexual intercourse in his life, and when—Christmas is the last day in *The Manticore*—he feels that he must decide between the values of Liesl and Johanna. David, the young scion of the Stauntons, had once said "that he hated Christmas more than any other day in the calendar" (*Fifth*, 170).

If David is to come to terms with Time it can only be by accepting the old temporal implications behind Christmas—"the two heads of Time at Sorgenfrei"—and incorporating the devil of his own and his family's past within his present self (*Manticore*, 305). On the Christmas Eve at Sorgenfrei, David begins his journal: "Was this the worst day in my life or the best? Both" (*Manticore*, 297). In helping him to come to terms with his "personal devil" as well as the "Old Devil"—she had done much the same for Dunstan (*Fifth*, 202-203)—Liesl had introduced David to the first cave that he had ever visited—a cave that is clearly within himself as well as within the mountains of the Tyrol. Liesl takes David both within the bowels of the earth and back into time when ancient men worshipped the bear. (In his own past, Felix, a stuffed bear, had been David's great solace when he was four and the first of as many as nine that he took to bed every night.) David felt "renewed ... and ... reborn" by the experience in the cave on the eve of Christmas, and on the following day Dunstan's Christmas gift was a gingerbread bear. Dunstan advised David to "make a working arrangement with the bear that lives within us." Liesl's gift was a watch "From the Brazen Head" with the mysterious traditional inscription: "Time is ... Time was ... Time is past" (*Manticore*, 303-308). If David is ever to live at Sorgenfrei he must—like Dunstan, Liesl, and Eisengrim—come to terms with the Devil that is Time.

The most time-oriented of the three inhabitants of Sorgenfrei has been Dunstan, a historian who epitomizes Deptford's servitude to Time. In his case, he was able to complement the diabolism of Time by a "lifelong involvement" with Mary Dempster, the saint in the image of Mary who seemed completely oblivious to both the time and the materialistic orientation of Deptford.

Liesl, too, comes from a time-oriented and materialistic Calvinist background. Her family had clearly profited from the American and Swiss automation of the clock-and-watch industry in the early nineteenth century, which virtually eliminated British watch production by 1860. Liesl's reaction had been more violent than Dunstan's. Herr Direktor Naegeli's priceless collection of clockwise automata was smashed to pieces by his heiress Liesl, who had "missed their charm and seen instead their awful rigidity and slavery to mechanical pattern" (*Wonders*, 314). After Liesl had been tamed by Eisengrim, she learned from him not merely how to come to terms with her past by reanimating within herself "the family knack of clockwork"

(*Manticore*, 285), but she also learned how to move, like Eisengrim, "through clockwork to the Magian World View" (*Wonders*, 323-324).

At Sorgenfrei, Eisengrim is clearly the first among equals. David Staunton feels that he "affects royal airs ... as the regulator of manners" (*Manticore*, 281). It is not merely that "his lifelong pose has been demonic" (*Wonders*, 149), or that like Liesl, he has taken a demonic name. Eisengrim had been liberated from time by the contempt for it he had "gained sitting inside Abdullah, when time had no significance." Yet, acting intuitively, as he seems always to have done, Eisengrim felt the need to empathize completely with the very clockwork that symbolized not only his own hell in Abdullah but also the hell of modern Western man. Eisengrim tells us: "I understand time. I mean my own time, as well as the clock's" (*Wonders*, 305).

We should do well, however, to note that Eisengrim seems to yearn only after old clockwork, and that for his repairs he required "seasoned metal— not new stuff" (*Wonders*, 312). This is particularly noticeable after his service as the double to that specialist in romance, Sir John Tresize. Romance is the quality which breaks the chains of Time. Marlowe's *Faust* comes to a climax in Act V precisely because Faust's fate is irrevocably sealed within ascertainable clock time. In Goethe's *Faust*, however, the seals of Time are broken by Gretchen's love.[12] Eisengrim's *Vision of Dr. Faustus* at the end of the *Soirée of Illusions* is based on this "romance" version of Faust's ascent to heaven after a full life of "striving" and "becoming," and despite his pact with Mephistopheles (*Fifth*, 182-183; *Wonders*, 337-339). Eisengrim defends to Ingstree (a member of the Cambridge Marlowe Society) just such a romance ending that Sir John Tresize wanted for his "Jekyll and Hyde" play: "A man redeemed and purged of evil by a woman's love." A romance, as Eisengrim reminds us, provides "a warm, safe place where Time hardly moves at all" (*Wonders*, 246-249, 252).

In conclusion, evil, as we have seen, has involved more and more the enslavement of modern man to Western technological progress. The clock is to a great extent both the symbol and the cause of that enslavement. In combining clockwork with romance Eisengrim had come to terms with the diabolism of Time—that was his magic.

UNIVERSITY OF VICTORIA

NOTES

A version of this paper was presented to the Association of Canadian University Teachers of English in May 1978.

[1] Christopher Marlowe, *Faustus*, ed. W. W. Greg (Oxford: Clarendon Press, 1950), A text, lines 1456-60.

2 Charles Baudelaire, "L'Horloge," *Les Fleurs du mal*, ed. Antoine Adam (Paris: Éditions Garnier Frères, 1959), pp. 87 and 374.

3 Alfred Tennyson, *The Devil and the Lady*, ed. Charles Tennyson (London: Macmillan, 1930), p. 21 (I.v).

4 Robertson Davies, *World of Wonders* (Toronto: Macmillan, 1975), p. 220.

5 Robertson Davies, *The Manticore* (Harmondsworth: Penguin, 1976), p. 68.

6 Robertson Davies, *Fifth Business* (New York: Signet, 1971), pp. 12, 15, 52, 105-06, *et passim*.

7 Henry D. Thoreau, *Walden*, ed. Walter Harding (New York: Twayne Publishers, Inc., 1962), p. 110.

8 Herman Melville, *Moby Dick* in *The Romances* (New York: Tudor Publishing Co., 1931), chs. 37 and 38.

9 The Willards—"several generations beginning with Benjamin about 1770" —were one of the most famous American families of clockmakers. They were known, among other things, for their "banjo" and musical clocks. See Cecil Clutton, G. H. Baillie, and C. A. Ilbert, eds., *Britten's Old Clocks and Watches and their Makers*, 8th edn. (New York: E. P. Dutton, 1973), p. 513.

10 Vaucanson, *An Account of the Mechanism of an Automaton....*, trans. J. T. Desaguliers (London: Stephen Varillon, 1742), Title Page.

11 See Bedini, "The Role of Automata in the History of Technology," *Technology and Culture*, 5 (1964), 39; and Diane Perrot, "*The Grotto* the Long Lost Automata by Jaquet Droz," *Antiquarian Horology*, 5 (December 1966), 170-172.

12 Further, Faust's "Vor mir den Tag und hinter mir die Nacht" clearly foreshadows the hegemony of heavenly light in Gretchen's "Noch blendet ihn der neue Tag." See Johann Wolfgang von Goethe, *Werke* (Hamburg: Christian Wegner, 1949), III, 40 and 363 (lines 1087 and 12093). Images of good and evil, priest and devil are also combined in Padre Blazon (see F. L. Radford, "Heinrich Heine, the Virgin, and the Hummingbird: *Fifth Business*—a Novel and its Subconscious," *English Studies in Canada*, 4 [Spring 1978], 97 and 110). There seem, however, to be no horological references relating to Blazon.

"People in Prominent Positions": A Study of the Public Figure in the Deptford Trilogy

David Monaghan

Fifth Business, I have suggested in an earlier paper, is flawed by Robertson Davies' failure to integrate the private and public aspects of Dunstan Ramsay's life drama.[1] What the novel claims is that there is a connection between Ramsay's "vital though never glorious" (*FB*, 14)[2] public role as Fifth Business, and his ability to be "a human, like other people" (*FB*, 201). Yet the qualities that characterize Ramsay as Fifth Business—curiosity, emotional detachment and a vindictive moralism—directly contradict those qualities of imagination, love and spirituality which he is eventually able to uncover within himself. The Ramsay who makes love to Liesl and thereby experiences "deep delight [and] such an aftermath of healing tenderness" (*FB*, 203) is simply not the same man who shortly afterwards, as Fifth Business, maliciously and gloatingly presides over Boy Staunton's fateful meeting with Magnus Eisengrim.

There is more at stake in this confusion than simply a blurring of Dunstan Ramsay's character, for implicit in Davies' argument that Ramsay has achieved a synthesis of private and public selves is an attempt to establish him as at least a partial emblem of the ideal towards which the entire Deptford trilogy strives. Interested as Davies undoubtedly is in Jungian psychology and as much as he stresses the individual's need to journey within in order to discover his unique self, he never loses sight of the fact that he must at the same time live in the world and play a public role.[3] Through Liesl he suggests, for example, that the greatness of Freud and Jung is not to be found in the body of work they have left behind them but in the heroism of their own lives during which they made "the inward journey while they were working like galley-slaves at their daily tasks" (*M*, 266). When he praises Freud and Jung for yoking together a public role with exploration of the self, Davies is not suggesting that their heroism derived merely from the fact that they possessed a Janus-like ability to look simultaneously inwards and outwards and that they would have achieved as much, if less meritoriously, had they been at liberty to escape daily cares and devote themselves entirely to contemplation of the self. On the contrary, Davies gives no evidence of believing that withdrawal from the world can produce anything better than a fool-saint like Mary Dempster. So far as he is concerned, the well-chosen public role will facilitate and indeed enlarge the inner journey. As Dunstan Ramsay says, his own—as winner of the Victoria Cross, symbol of heroism—and the king's roles as public icons, give them "obligations above what is merely personal" (*FB*, 79). Freud and Jung, then, deserve admiration because they chose appropriately and, as a consequence, were able to achieve an unusual degree of self-knowledge.

Davies' admiration for the individual who manages to integrate public and private selves is intensified by an acute awareness of the ways in which the public role can divert him away from rather than towards self-knowledge. For all of us, the role that we play before the world is in part a mask— hence Dr. von Haller, the Jungian analyst, calls it our Persona. However, there are those for whom the mask conceals the self not only from others but also from themselves: "We all create an outward self with which to face the world, and some people come to believe that is what they truly are. . . . That is why they are such poor specimens when they are caught without their masks on. They have lived chiefly through the Persona" (*M*, 228-29).

The Persona which each person chooses will, then, according to Davies, either obscure or illuminate the inner self. However, the choice which faces everyone is particularly significant for famous people because, in the process of achieving fame, they must inevitably develop public selves of unusually large proportions. Therefore, in deciding to put at the centre of his novels characters who have acquired some degree of worldly reputation, Davies was providing himself with particularly good opportunities for revealing the full implications of the question of public roles. Dunstan Ramsay is well-known amongst religious scholars and even tourists. Denyse Hornick, for example, knows of his interest in saints because "my books were not easy to overlook if one was in the travel business" (*FB*, 215). Boy Staunton has become famous enough in the fields of business and politics to merit an obituary in *Neue Zürcher Zeitung*, a Swiss newspaper that, "like the London *Times*, recognizes only the most distinguished achievements of the Angel of Death" (*WW*, 304). David Staunton is "an eminent advocate" (*M*, 24). And Magnus Eisengrim is "the greatest magician in the world" (*WW*, 8). Boy and Magnus are clearly much more famous than either David or Ramsay, but all have one essential thing in common: their Personae are sufficiently impressive to have won the admiration of large numbers of people who fall outside their circle of personal acquaintances and who know them entirely as Businessman/Politician, Magician, Lawyer, and Hagiologist respectively. This means that they are in particular danger of lapsing into the supreme egotism of believing that their masks comprise their entire reality. However, since their public selves operate on such a large scale it also means that, if they have been well chosen, they can provide a cloak capacious enough to contain within it an unusually extensive exploration of the private self.

Dunstan Ramsay, as I have already pointed out, is intended to stand as an example of the man who achieves an integration of public and private selves. However, Davies' attempt to demonstrate the nature of this integration in *Fifth Business* is not entirely convincing. Neither does Ramsay become any more convincing as a result of his appearances in the second and third parts of the Deptford trilogy. In *The Manticore* he seems very much to be the product of Leisl's teaching. David perceives in him "a new geniality" (*M*, 247), and Ramsay himself gives evidence of increased self-knowledge: "your mother once asked me to make love to her, and I refused. In spite of one very great example I had in my life I couldn't rise to love as an act of charity" (*M*, 262). However, the Ramsay that we encounter in *World of Wonders* is closer to his Fifth Business self. His main interest in Eisengrim's story is that he should win immortality as its recorder: "I'm making a record—a document.... When we're all gone ... there may be a few who will still prove a point with 'Ramsay says...'" (*WW*, 316). To aspire to immortality is, for Davies, as he reveals through his analysis of Boy Staunton, one of the grossest forms of egotism. Ramsay's repeated meanness in financial matters and his stated preference for the document over artistic truth (*WW*, 60) further suggest a man who is guided by his original Calvinist social milieu and the rational faculty, and not by feeling or imagination. Can we then say that any of Davies' other public figures provide him with an objective correlative for his ideal of the fully realized human being?

Boy Staunton obviously does not, and neither is he intended to. As conceived by Davies, Boy is the example *par excellence* of the man who "lived chiefly through the Persona." Ramsay can see so little evidence of his Deptford roots in Staunton's adult self that to him it seems that Boy has "made himself out of nothing" (*FB*, 100) and that "he was always the quintessence of something that somebody else had recognized and defined" (*FB*, 103). Ultimately Boy becomes entirely swallowed up in his public role and arrives at no more self-knowledge than that, as Lieutenant Governor, "I would be no more than the animation of that uniform, or some version of it" and that "I have lost my freedom of choice" (*WW*, 310). Lacking any core of inner reality upon which to base his actions, Boy can escape the consequences of the trap into which he has placed himself only by following the example of his original hero, the Prince of Wales: "He was going to abdicate, like his hero before him. But unlike his Prince of Wales he didn't mean to live to face the world afterward" (*WW*, 312).

In David Staunton and Magnus Eisengrim, however, we are presented with characters who come closer to embodying Davies' ideal. *The Manticore*, in fact, traces only those parts of David's life during which he achieves an understanding of the extent to which the role of lawyer has become his entire reality. However, we are left with a clear sense that in the future David might undertake the heroic task of journeying within and might seek a new public role that will facilitate this private exploration. *World of Wonders* goes further than *The Manticore*, and in its final pages Davies argues that Magnus has become a full human being, a man who has developed a public role as the Mephistophelean magician that has brought him into touch with his wolfish shadow, and which has assisted him in developing a Magian World View. Unfortunately, we cannot be entirely satisfied with this conclusion for—as presented in *Fifth Business*, *The Manticore* and most of *World of Wonders*—Magnus is no more than a fascinating study of someone who, like Boy Staunton, is entirely a public figure.[4] The two versions of Magnus Eisengrim appear to be irreconcilable and we are left with a character who is confusing rather than, as Davies clearly intended, richly ambiguous.

Neither David Staunton nor Magnus Eisengrim, then, can be taken in any simple sense as an emblem of the ideal integration of private and public selves. Nevertheless, an examination of their development which takes full account of the limitations, both deliberate and accidental, in Davies' presentation of them can cast considerable light on the vision of human potentiality that informs the entire Deptford trilogy.

David Staunton, perhaps not surprisingly considering he is the son of Boy Staunton, has tried to make his public role his only reality. Why this is so emerges under analysis. In the account that he gives to Dr. von Haller of his childhood and adolescence David reveals a number of personal problems. He is troubled above all by his relationship with his father, a man whose approval he feels he can win only by achieving a certain type of manhood: "I cared whether he thought I was a worthy person—a man—a proper person to be his son" (*M*, 48). Almost equally important, though, is the turmoil into which he is thrown as a consequence of the unsuccessful termination of his relationship with Judy Wolff. Having committed himself once to a world controlled by feelings and having found it so unpredictable and painful, David is suspicious of giving any further credence to the promptings

48

of his emotions. A similar tendency to withdraw in disgust follows David's first experience of evil in the shape of Bill Unsworth, who induces him to participate in the motiveless vandalizing of an unoccupied cabin, a process which Unsworth completes by defecating on the family photographs.

Had David tried to come to terms with these problems he might well have set himself on the path to becoming the feeling and self-knowing individual that is Davies' ideal. However, when he discovered the law, David also believed that he had discovered a way of denying any obligation to look within himself. As a lawyer, David is provided with a Persona that allows him to impress and rival his father while avoiding any direct encounter with him: "In fact, you created a romantic Persona that successfully rivalled that of the rich, sexually adventurous Boy Staunton without ever challenging him on his own ground?" (*M*, 234). Furthermore, he is entering a field in which, far from being directed to come to terms with his feelings, he is instructed as to their irrelevance. Pargetter, David's law tutor at Oxford and his "father in art" (*M*, 198), tells him that if he is to master even one branch of the law he must "put [his] emotions in cold storage" (*M*, 196). Nothing could be more welcome to David than this advice: "I wanted the law because I wanted to master something in which I would know where I stood and which would not be open to the whims and preconceptions of people like Louis Wolff" (*M*, 195). The law and its attendant rituals, for which he has great admiration, provide David with a rational framework that comes to embody all that is true, even though this truth involves no more than "to render to everyone his due" (*M*, 60). Thus, he is able to argue, "Nor did I like the dream-interpretation game, which contradicted every rule of evidence known to me; the discovery of truth is one of the principal functions of the law, to which I have given the best that is in me; is truth to be found in the vapours of dreams?" (*M*, 22). Finally, the law gives David a way of dealing with the evil that he saw in Bill Unsworth without in any sense coming to terms with it or acknowledging it as a part of himself: "I was against whatever it was that possessed him, and I thought the law was the best way of making my opposition effective" (*M*, 155). Even when forced to defend people like Jimmy Veale, whom he considers evil, David is able to maintain his distance: "I was always aware that I stood very near to the power of evil when I undertook the cases that brought me the greatest part of my reputation. . . . I like the struggle. . . . I am like a man who has built his house on the lip of a volcano" (*M*, 228). Evil, therefore, becomes something David either fights or flirts with, but not something he believes he has any obligation to understand.

49

However, much as David Staunton's public role enables him to deny the need to journey within the self, he is unable to make it his entire reality. He is thus left with a neglected inner self which, inevitably according to Jung, makes itself felt in a disruptive way. The result is a nervous breakdown that takes him into therapy with Dr. von Haller. Liesl questions the value of the therapeutic process but, if nothing else, it brings David to an understanding of the damage he has done himself by making his Persona operate entirely as an "armour" (*M*, 229).[5] As a result he is ready to begin the journey inwards upon which Liesl is determined to lead him. In order for David to become a modern hero, "the man who conquers in the inner struggle" (*M*, 268), Liesl believes that he needs to experience the awe of religious feeling, and thus she takes him to the ancient temple of bear worship, deep within the side of a mountain. Although things do not work out as Liesl anticipates —David is not at all impressed by the bear relics—she does achieve her goal. On the journey back David, exhausted and terrified by a sudden roar of wind, is forced to search within himself for the strength to go on. The exploration puts him in touch with the spirit of his heroically independent great-grandmother, Maria Ann Dymock, and he completes the journey. As a consequence of this experience David Staunton feels reborn.

By the end of *The Manticore*, then, David Staunton is well on the way to being a complete human being. He has come to recognize the limits of his public role, and he has begun to uncover the reality of his inner self. Unfortunately, by stopping where he does, Davies gives us no sense of how David will go about the crucial task of finding a new Persona capable of nurturing and enhancing his attempt to become completely human. Certainly, whatever form it might take, it will have to embody the spirit of Maria Ann Dymock rather than Pargetter or Boy Staunton. The Lawyer Persona may be adaptable. Even Pargetter has admitted that the law gives the imagination scope (*M*, 207) and, if David is willing to return and defend Matey Quelch, whom he now recognizes as his Shadow, it may lead him into a meaningful encounter with evil. But this can only be speculation. Clearly depicted as David Staunton is, he remains a character who has only the potential to embody Davies' ideal of the completely integrated human being, and he does not provide us with any insight into how this integration can be achieved.

Davies proceeds further with the life drama of Magnus Eisengrim, but ultimately he is perhaps less illuminating than David Staunton. We may be frustrated by Davies' early termination of his account of David Staunton's search for the self, but at least we are left with a sense that we understand the character as presented, and can make some predictions about the direction his life might take in the future. Magnus Eisengrim, on the other hand, is, like Dunstan Ramsay before him, a confusing character. What the author claims Eisengrim finally becomes—a man whose public role as the Mephistophelean magician has brought him into touch with his wolfish Shadow—is inconsistent with the entirely public figure revealed earlier. In my examination of Dunstan Ramsay, I paid particular attention to Davies' use of two central metaphors, the boy and Fifth Business, since his depiction of Ramsay's inner journey was structured around the boy, and his depiction of Ramsay's public role was structured around Fifth Business. It was in his failure to reconcile the two metaphors, as I argued, that Davies lost control of his character and of his larger thematic point. A similar confusion of metaphors is to be found in *World of Wonders*, and the novel can be usefully approached by considering the implications of "a bottle in the smoke" and the Wolf, both images through which Magnus Eisengrim is defined.

The analogy between Magnus Eisengrim and "A Bottle in the Smoke," which is the title of the first section of *World of Wonders*, is explained by Magnus himself: "A verse from the Book of Psalms kept running through my head that seemed to me to describe my state perfectly. 'I am become like a bottle in the smoke.' ... It means one of those old wineskins the Hebrews used; it means a goatskin that has been scraped out, and tanned, and blown up, and hung over the fire till it is as hard as a warrior's boot. That was how I saw myself" (*WW*, 134-35). According to this metaphor, then, Magnus is a completely public person, one who has assimilated all experience into the hardening of his social skin (or "armour" as Dr. von Haller would have put it), with the result that his inner self remains empty.

As he appears in *Fifth Business* and *The Manticore*, Magnus is entirely consistent with the image of "a bottle in the smoke." In *Fifth Business*, Magnus tells Ramsay that it is essential to the success of his magic show that Magnus Eisengrim not simply be his stage Persona: "the show must keep its character all the time. I must not be seen off the stage except under circumstances that carry some *cachet.* ... When people meet me I must be always the distinguished gentleman conferring a distinction; not a nice fellow, just like the rest of the boys" (*FB*, 186). Later he denies any continuing connection with his original Paul Dempster self: "My real name is Magnus Eisengrim; that is who I am and that is how the world knows me. But before I found out who I was, I was called Paul Dempster" (*FB*, 231). This denial is repeated in *The Manticore* during a discussion of *Phantasmata*, the "autobiography" of Magnus Eisengrim composed by Dunstan Ramsay: " ... it is truer to the essence of my life than the dowdy facts could ever be. Do you understand? I am what I have made myself—the greatest

51

illusionist since Moses and Aaron. Do the facts suggest or explain what I am? No: but Ramsay's book does. I am truly Magnus Eisengrim. The illusion, the lie, is a Canadian called Paul Dempster" (*M*, 260).

For much of *World of Wonders* Davies' intention appears to be to explain how such a completely public person as Magnus Eisengrim was created, and to this end he examines in detail the process by which Paul Dempster simply ceased to exist. Like David Staunton, Paul has some investment in escaping from his real self. His early years, spent with a sternly Calvinistic father and a mother the village boys have labelled "hoor," were painful ones. However, on his own it is unlikely that he would have been any more successful than David in entirely erasing the self. Paul's experiences with Willard and Sir John Tresize are responsible for this.

Once he has been abducted by Willard, Paul enters a world in which no one acknowledges him as a person: "Willard and Charlie . . . talked about me as though I had no ears to hear them, and no understanding" (*WW*, 52). Being "Nobody" (56), Paul can achieve identity only as the "soul of Abdullah" (50), the card-playing automaton inside which he sits ten hours a day until he is seventeen or eighteen: "Abdullah was the face I presented to the world" (*WW*, 110).

Because his personality has been totally absorbed into Abdullah, Paul returns to being "a *tabula rasa*" and "a dear, sweet little zero" (*WW*, 168), as Lady Tresize calls him, once he escapes his enslavement to the machine. And as such he is prey to a repetition of the exploitation that he suffered at the hands of Willard. The Tresizes want him in their theatrical company precisely because, as a Nobody, he can be easily shaped into Sir John's double. The parallels between these two stages in Paul's experience are made quite explicit: "Try to get inside Sir John! Was this to be another Abdullah?" (*WW*, 172).

By the time he completes his apprenticeship as Mungo Fetch, the double, Davies' hero has entirely lost touch with his original Paul Dempster self. Therefore, in finally creating a Persona for himself he can do no more than take elements from his two earlier roles; Magnus Eisengrim is a grotesque combination of the art of Abdullah and the style of Sir John Tresize. By making this particular synthesis Magnus would appear to have rejected that one aspect of Sir John—his dedication to the theatre of feeling—which held promise of spiritual insight in favour of the fake marvels of conjuring, a "gaffed" (*WW*, 62-63) art. Since Magnus Eisengrim is so entirely a Public Figure—at least as much so as Boy Staunton—and since this Persona has its roots in deception, scorn for humanity and vanity, it is not surprising that Davies attributes to him extreme versions of the vices to which those who come to identify entirely with their masks fall prey. Above all, Magnus is an egotist. This is David Staunton's overwhelming impression of him—"What an egotist!" (*M*, 258)—and also Ramsay's: "Magnus Eisengrim ... had a full share, a share pressed down and overflowing, of the egotism of the theatre artist. Who could not bear the least slight; who expected, as of right, to be served first at table, and to go through all doors first" (*WW*, 11). Magnus also shares with Boy Staunton a spiteful vengefulness that, at least according to Ramsay's analysis of Staunton's "stone-in-the-snowball" (*FB*, 235) mentality, is an inevitable offspring of a solipsistic world view. This emerges first in his refusal to allow his former tormentor Willard to die: "Yes, gentlemen, it was Revenge, and it was sweet" (*WW*, 132). Vengefulness is also evident in Magnus' manipulation of the account of his life in order to humiliate his old enemy, Roger Ingestree. But its most significant manifestation is in the "murder" of Boy Staunton, the man responsible for his premature birth and unhappy early childhood.

So far so good, but unfortunately this account of Magnus Eisengrim as "a bottle in the smoke" is not at all consistent with the Magnus who suddenly emerges in the last fifty pages or so of *World of Wonders*. The process of revision is begun by Liesl who characterizes Magnus, whom she first encountered mending toys at Sorgenfrei, as a very different person than the one I have described. According to Liesl, Magnus' public roles as magician and member of Sir John Tresize's theatre of feeling have brought him deep inner knowledge, so much so that he possesses "the Magian World View" which she defines as "a sense of the unfathomable wonder of the invisible world that existed side by side with a hard recognition of the roughness and cruelty and day-to-day demands of the tangible world" (*WW*, 287). Magnus, who, we must remember, has just given an account of his life shaped by the spirit of the "bottle in the smoke" metaphor, now begins to support Liesl's claims by defining himself as the Wolf. Wolfishness according to Magnus is his Shadow, which he has not only recognized but also made part of his Persona—Eisengrim means wolf. By so doing he has created a public role capable of reinforcing his search for self-knowledge, and has thereby achieved full humanness. Thus, he tells Ramsay, "I am a more complete human being than you are" (*WW*, 301), and offers in support of his claim: "I took the name [Eisengrim], and recognized the fact, and thereby got it up out of my depths so that at least I could be aware of it and take a look at it, now and then. I won't say I domesticated the wolf, but I knew where his lair was, and what he might do" (*WW*, 306).

Davies clearly recognizes the discrepancies between his two pictures of Magnus Eisengrim and makes an attempt to reconcile them by means of a debate between Magnus and Ramsay. Ramsay, here voicing the reader's thoughts, argues that Magnus is in the grip of a vengeful spirit and so cannot be as mature a human being as he professes. By way of rebuttal, Magnus claims that he simply toyed with Ingestree when he happened to cross his path and, rather than revenging himself on Boy Staunton, he was no more than an observer as the Great Justice exacted its penalty from him: "So— here was a situation when it was clear to me that the Great Justice had called the name of Boy Staunton. Was it for me to hold him back?" (*WW*, 314). Magnus' account of his part in Boy's death is in itself feasible enough, especially given our knowledge of Boy's burgeoning death wish. However, he simply fails to give a convincing enough explanation for his treatment of Willard and Ingestree to dispel our sense that his is a vengeful and hence an egotistical personality. In fact, no explanation at all is offered for his treatment of Willard and his contention that he merely gave Ingestree "a smart clout" (*WW*, 313) when "he [came] back into my life by chance" (*WW*, 302), does not fit the facts. The narrative through which Magnus gains his revenge on Ingestree does indeed begin as a result of an opportune circumstance that brings his old enemy to Sorgenfrei. However, in order that it might be completed in front of an audience sufficiently prestigious to ensure Ingestree's complete humiliation Magnus has to travel from Switzerland to London.

At the end of their debate, Ramsay is fully satisfied and now calls Magnus an egoist, a term that Magnus himself has earlier distinguished from egotist: "An egotist is a self-absorbed creature, delighted with himself. . . . But an egoist, like Sir John, is a much more serious being, who makes himself, his instincts, yearning and tastes the touchstone of every experience. The world, truly, is his creation" (*WW*, 172). But we cannot be so easily satisfied, and not only because Magnus' defence against the charge of vengefulness has been unconvincing. Other important considerations have been entirely passed over.

If, for example, Magnus has become a complete human being, why does Davies go to so much trouble earlier to distinguish between Sir John Tresize's dedication to romantic theatre—a true art that is for him, as was opera for Monica Gall in *A Mixture of Frailties*, a vehicle for learning about feelings —and Magnus' dedication to the fake art of conjuring? The magician, as described by David Staunton, who has good knowledge of such matters since he strove to be "a magician of the courtroom" (*M*, 55), is a man whose success depends on keeping people "in awe of him, and at a distance" (*M*, 258) in order that they might be tricked more easily. Given this definition of the art of the magician, and it is fully borne out in Davies' account of

Wanless' World of Wonders, the links that Liesl claims to exist between the "unfathomable wonder" of the Magian World Vision and the illusion of wonder created by the conjurer, evaporate completely.

Even if we were willing to overlook such confusions, however, we would still be left with the central problem of resolving the novel's two central metaphors. If Magnus Eisengrim is "a bottle in the smoke," an entirely public figure bearing no trace of Paul Dempster, as he frequently claims, how can he have explored down into his self and discovered his wolfish shadow? By his own definition, Magnus is a Phantasmata, a vision or an illusion; he has no self to explore and hence no Shadow.

At the centre of each novel in the Deptford trilogy, then, is a character who strives for the integration of public and private selves that is Davies' ideal. Davies takes David Staunton only part way along the journey towards self-knowledge, but Dunstan Ramsay and Magnus Eisengrim are presented as characters who have had considerable success in their pursuit of maturity. Neither character, though, is entirely convincing in that Davies is unable to integrate all the complex elements at work in their personalities. Thus, rich ambiguity is replaced by a degree of confusion. This is not to deny, though, that the Deptford trilogy provides considerable insight into some central issues of human personality. Davies' analysis of the ways in which the Persona can overwhelm the rest of the personality is masterly, and through his sometimes certain and sometimes faltering analysis of the development of Dunstan Ramsay, David Staunton and Magnus Eisengrim he increases the reader's awareness of the proper relationship that should exist between public and private selves.

MOUNT SAINT VINCENT UNIVERSITY

NOTES

[1] "Metaphors and Confusions," *Canadian Literature*, 67 (Winter, 1976), 64-73.

[2] All references to the novels of Robertson Davies will be cited in the text of my essay, and the following editions and abbreviations used: *Fifth Business* (New York: Signet, 1971), *FB*; *The Manticore* (Harmondsworth: Penguin, 1977), *M*; *World of Wonders* (Harmondsworth; Penguin, 1977), *WW*.

[3] Even a strictly Jungian approach to Davies' novels should of course be sufficient to deal with his interest in public roles because it could approach the topic through the notion of the Persona. Jungians, however, have mainly focused on the inner journey. Among the most illuminating have been Peter Baltensperger, "Battles with the Trolls," *Canadian Literature*, 71 (Winter, 1976), 59-67; Marilyn Chapman, "Female Archetypes in

Fifth Business," *Canadian Literature,* 80 (Spring, 1979), 131-38; Gordon Roper, "Robertson Davies' *Fifth Business* and 'that Old Fantastical Duke of Dark Corners, C. G. Jung'," *Journal of Canadian Fiction,* 1 (Winter, 1972), 33-39.

4 Other critics do not seem to have noticed the inconsistencies in Davies' treatment of Magnus Eisengrim, but rather have chosen one or other of Davies' mutually exclusive versions of the character as representing the author's intentions. Thus, Nancy E. Bjerring, "Deep in the Old Man's Puzzle," *Canadian Literature,* 62 (Autumn, 1974), 59, argues that Magnus has lost contact with humanity and is absorbed in self-aggrandisement, while Russell M. Brown and Donna A. Bennett, "Magnus Eisengrim: The Shadow of the Trickster in the Novels of Robertson Davies," *Modern Fiction Studies,* 22 (1976), 360, see him as having fully integrated the mind and the Shadow in a way that enables him to escape one-sidedness.

5 Patricia Monk, "Psychology and Myth in *The Manticore,*" *Studies in Canadian Literature,* 2 (1977), 69-81, offers a detailed if not altogether convincing analysis of Davies' ambivalence towards Jungian theory in *The Manticore.*

The (Auto)-Biographical Compulsions of Dunstan Ramsay

Patricia Merivale

Insofar as *Fifth Business* is Dunstan Ramsay's autobiography, its narrative structures may be fruitfully analyzed in terms of a probable source in C. G. Jung's *Memories, Dreams, Reflections*.[1] Insofar as it is Dunstan's "lives" of his "saints," it seems more useful to investigate possible connections with a whole group of texts: Hugh MacLennan's *The Watch That Ends the Night*,[2] and Thomas Mann's *Dr. Faustus*—both especially relevant examples of the fictional genre, the "elegiac romance,"[3] to which I see *Fifth Business* as belonging—and Thomas Mann's ironic Saint's Life, *The Holy Sinner*, all help to elucidate the parodic complex of theme and structure in *Fifth Business*, and to support my general contention that the Deptford Trilogy is built upon a dialectic of intertextuality, which swings not only between Deptford and Zürich (as has been pointed out), or between "realism" and "romance," but more specifically between MacLennan's sort of book and Mann's.

The elegiac romance is a grouping of (chiefly) Anglo-American novels in which the narrator, allegedly telling the story of his much-admired dead friend, turns out in the end to be telling his own story, in terms of his relationship with his hero, and of his transcending, through the very act of narration, the now dead hero's influence. Several such novels, but in particular Scott Fitzgerald's *The Great Gatsby* and Robert Penn Warren's *All the King's Men*, provide useful analogues and probable sources for Davies, either directly, or perhaps indirectly, through MacLennan.

There are numerous Canadian elegiac romances: Earle Birney's "David" illustrates the pastoral and elegiac aspects of the form, and bears the same sort of analogous relationship to MacLennan as Milton's *Lycidas* does to, say, *The Great Gatsby*. Robert Kroetsch's *The Studhorse Man* and A. M. Klein's *The Second Scroll*, along with (in more tangled form) Leonard Cohen's *Beautiful Losers*, make up a brilliant but less characteristic group of self-reflexive texts—explicitly Canadian artist-parables—flaunting artifice in the manner of Nabokov's elegiac romances, rather than Warren's or Fitzgerald's.

But it is true of elegiac romances in general, as of the Canadian texts I have named, that they are indeed "elegiac," in that a first-person narrator is under a sort of biographical compulsion to tell us the story of a person now dead, while adopting for himself, in varying degrees, the narrative posture of an unironic pane of window-glass: "I'm not very interesting. But let me tell you about my marvelous dead friend. . . . " They are all romances, in that the hero is a little larger and more splendid than the conventions of psychological realism encourage, while the narrator subdues his own characterization to those same conventions. We come to see that the "hero," as described to us, is largely a projection into mythic dimensions of the needs and obsessions of the narrator, and that the apparent biographic compulsion is more truly an autobiographic one. The story is not so much the hero's as the narrator's: how he shared the hero's life, survived his death, and is now providing an elegiac memorial for him, in order that he, the narrator, may finally free himself from the burden of his obsession, come to know himself more truly, and renew his own existence on better terms: "Tomorrow to fresh woods, and pastures new" (Milton). "That day, the last of my youth, on the last of our mountains" (Birney).

There is a "doubleness" in such a narrative which borders on duplicity, and there is a built-in unreliability in such a narrator. For the story of a dead man, in the past, is being re-shaped, for the purposes of a living man, in the present; past experience becomes the "present" of the narrative process itself.

More specifically, Davies and MacLennan are working, like Warren, Fitzgerald, and the Bellow of *Humboldt's Gift* (with Ford, Conrad and many others in the background) within the norms of psychological realism imbued with an almost documentary sense of place, historical context, and men at work. Davies' and MacLennan's elegiac romances, like the Anglo-American ones, are based on a "male bonding" relationship between mythically heightened hero and idealizing narrator, often in uneven competition for the same woman, in uneasy equilibrium among love, hatred and indifference. The narrator is often, like Bob in Birney's "David," or like Dunstan, to say the least of it complicit in the hero's death; he concludes his doubled narrative with a transcendent affirmation of his hard-won identity.

The dead heroes, figuratively, need to be buried twice (as does Bellow's Humboldt, quite literally). They haunt the interstices between the event and its narration, exercising power still over the narrator—until he can bury them again by solving the puzzle of their deaths, thus integrating them, through the aesthetic epiphany of his narration, into his continuing life. These heroes leave a heavy legacy to their admirers, heavier even than the wearying manuscript which constitutes Humboldt's gift (or bequest). Mac-Lennan's Jerome leaves George the burden of Catherine.

Mrs. Dempster's legacy is only the box with her ashes in: "I have always been meaning to put them in some proper place," says Dunstan (*FB*, 235). Boy Staunton's legacy, the stone, is made still heavier and more disquieting by its weight of Jungian significance. It is evidently the stone of Ramsay's secret self, and thus corresponds to the stone which the ten-year-old C. G. Jung put into a pencil-case, along with a tiny carved mannikin, and concealed in his attic for many years (*Memories, Dreams, Reflections*, p. 21). Paul Dempster, born prematurely (in Dunstan's tenth year) as a result of Staunton's casting of that stone, resembles not only that mannikin "put . . . in the pencil case, where I made him a little bed. I even made a coat for him out of a bit of wool" (*MDR*, 21), but also Jung's baby sister, whose birth (when Jung was nine) is described a few pages later: "a red, shrunken face like an old man's . . . a few single long red hairs" (*MDR*, 25). Davies evidently conflates the two episodes: Paul, "red . . . wrinkled like a tiny old man . . . covered with weedy long black hair" is put into a "nest . . . of jeweller's cotton and hot-water bottles" and fed with "a glass fountain-pen filler" (*FB*, 19). Starting from these rather exact borrowings, one could speculate further on the ways in which the narrative structure of *Fifth Business* corresponds to that of Jung's own psychobiography: both books focus on the significant revelations, in extreme old age, of concealed or suppressed childhood secrets involving a mannikin and "*his*" (*MDR*, 21) stone—secrets kept (apart from oblique references—*FB*, 11, 93, *MDR*, 117, 174) for sixty and seventy-three years respectively. "My entire youth can be understood in terms of this secret" (*MDR*, 41): Jung could be speaking for Dunstan as well as for himself.

The stones, while both central to the autobiographies, do not mean quite the same thing. Dunstan must, towards the very end of his life, "feel [his] strength returning in this house among the mountains" (of Jung's part of Switzerland: *FB*, 14), before he can dispose of the stone of his complicity and guilt, which stone indeed is like "the secret story . . . the rock against which [the patient] is shattered . . . a key to the treatment," which lies at the beginning of any Jungian analysis (*MDR*, 117). Staunton's drowned body, like so many others floating to the surfaces of Canadian fictions, can only be truly re-buried (and the stone cast away) when his death can be accounted for; thus, at long last, the stone can become as secure a part of Dunstan's identity as Jung's stone was, from the very beginning, of his.

Explicit in MacLennan, as well as in Davies, is a more general pattern of death-and-resurrection. Dunstan Ramsay, presumed dead in the trenches of

World War I (in which MacLennan's Jerome Martell also was wounded),
revives into a new name and identity; Martell, another Enoch Arden, comes
back from the dead after World War II with a rather implausible new line
in saintliness. Evidently the historical panorama (1917-1950) is one layer of
these heroes' specifically Canadian relevance. Another layer is an affirmation
of national identity, like those found in *All the King's Men*, *The Great
Gatsby*—and Mann's *Dr. Faustus*—through the quasi-allegorical status of
each pair: the narrator, seeing the nation in his hero, is then able to embody
it in himself.

The wounds and resurrections are part of the heroes' more general mythic
relevance; as Fisher-Kings, as Canadian Percivals, they are clearly part of a
fertility-sterility pattern seen in each book as the usually erotic triangle of
two men and a woman. But that these heroes have much in common as
personifications of mythic heroism, as parts of an allegorical view of Canadian identity, and as "realistic" examples of Canadian heroic careers through
the two world wars, is not in itself the point of elegiac romance. The
narrators, George Stewart and Dunstan Ramsay, choose or need to see
Jerome Martell, Boy Staunton (and Mrs. Dempster) in their heroic, mythic
dimension, while seeing themselves as younger, subservient, less vivid, more
ignorant—and as much more concerned about the heroes than the heroes
ever seem to be about them. "Brilliant young men [like Boy Staunton] seem
to need a dull listener [like me]" says Dunstan (*FB*, 99). Both narrators are
trapped by what Ramsay calls "their need" for saints (*FB*, 163)—and they
themselves are window glass rather than stained glass. Yet they are permitted
to develop, while their heroes, like stained glass, stay marvellously the same.

If Tennyson's *Enoch Arden* had been narrated by Philip Ray, the second
husband, it would be an elegiac romance. Our narrators tend to be Philip
Rays, "ordinary" men who do not turn their powers of projection and
idealization upon themselves, and who tend, sexually as in other ways, to be
the weak knee of these erotic triangles. In MacLennan's novel, George
Stewart, although he is Catherine's second husband, was her first suitor; he
lacked the forcefulness to take her when opportunity offered. Poor George—
the first half of the book is an extended periphrasis for "poor George"—finds
her again, married to Jerome; he hangs about, a bachelor schoolmaster
friend, the sort of man one can trust one's wife with. Admiration for Jerome
at least as much as friendship and muted love for Catherine holds George,
the weakest angle, in the triangle: "In those days I had no inner authority
against a man I had installed as a substitute father"; "I knew nothing then
of this world of pressure and politics and all I could do was listen"; Jerome
was "the most attractive male animal in Montreal"; "I was determined to

60

permit myself no jealousy of Jerome," (*WN*, 272, 164, 150, 121, 232) and so forth. Jerome abandons Catherine to George's care; he "dies"; they marry; Jerome returns from the dead, and George's report thereof nearly kills Catherine, the life-long invalid, the heavy responsibility. Jerome, always a healer, and by now a messianic bringer of religious comfort as well, saves her life and then leaves the couple for "a job out West," dead at last, at least to George's consciousness. By the logic of the narrative structure, we presume that George, the ideal second husband, will, like Warren's Jack Burden, whom he resembles in several ways, survive them both.

Robertson Davies requires four characters to carry all the qualities that MacLennan packed into the perhaps somewhat overcrowded character of Jerome, and four (male-male-female) triangles to provide congruence with MacLennan's one. Jerome's healing genius throughout and his later saintly qualities go to Mrs. Dempster and Liesl; his social and political glamour, his knowledge of "pressure and politics," his irresponsibility as a husband, his philandering, go to Boy Staunton; his "mythic" boyhood, with his flight, aged ten, from a darkness to a deeper darkness, to a new name and a new life, fleeing from the sexual encounter of a promiscuous and nearly-mad mother with a nameless, lower-caste brute, which encounters result, in MacLennan at once, in Davies in the long run, in the death of the mother —all this goes to Paul Dempster. Jerome's qualities as a trickster hero go to Paul's later avatar, Magnus Eisengrim, the one colossal figure in Dunstan's well-stocked gallery of "saints." All these characters are in one way or another "new-born," or twice-buried, or at least re-named.

Dunstan takes on himself Jerome's heroic soldiering in France; Jerome's leg wound becomes an amputation, and he acquires at once the weals on back and side for which Jerome must await the Nazi torture-chambers; but hyperbole goes the other way, as he modestly reduces Jerome's eleven bayonet victims to three revolver victims. Dunstan then becomes more a "watcher of life from the sidelines" (*FB*, 198), a Stewart-like bachelor friend and celibate schoolmaster, a husband-surrogate to whom Boy cannot even succeed in handing over his wife. Dunstan, who, like George, had once courted her, fastidiously refuses the task. In each of three erotic triangles, Dunstan is weak-kneed; to Boy, with Leola; to Eisengrim, with Faustina and then Liesl. Only in the triangle of responsibility for Mrs. Dempster does he seem dominant; but here too he is taking on, on the one hand, the guilt that Boy has either never acknowledged or conveniently forgotten—the stone—and on the other hand, the filial resposibility that Paul Dempster has escaped from and Magnus Eisengrim only cursorily acknowledged—the ashes. This guilt and responsibility start at the time of Paul's birth, which caused Mrs.

Dempster's madness, but become no lighter when she dies many years later, for Dunstan knows that he has contributed to that, too, by his careless revelation that Paul is still alive.

It should be clear by now that I doubt if the parallels of plot and structure between *The Watch That Ends the Night* and *Fifth Business* are pure coincidence. Davies could have found the basic structure in dozens of other familiar and available elegiac romances, including *Dr. Faustus,* or even invented it anew, but he did not in fact need to do more than follow Mac-Lennan's example, as numerous other similarities suggest that he did. It may be that Davies' admiration for what he saw as "the most Canadian of novels"[4] prompted him both to a conscious tribute to and a subversive spoof of MacLennan's book. Or perhaps he hoped to go MacLennan one better, to provide more "marvelous" versions of the ordinary, unconsciously saintly Canadian who stays home—George Stewart—and of the flamboyantly mythical Canadian who travels abroad a lot—Jerome Martell.

Dunstan is the most ironic and sharply critical of elegiac narrators, as Boy is the least magnetic of dead heroes; Dunstan is even ironic about his own rather odd and unconvincing obsession with Boy; he excuses it as curiosity, but knows that he is also drawn by the glamorous power of a sub-Gatsby ("a Scott Fitzgerald character," as he says: *FB,* 103). But obsessed he still is, and continues to be, as his stone paperweight bears witness, until the end of *World of Wonders,* when, with the responsibility for Boy's death more evenly distributed, Dunstan can free himself by telling, in these two books, the "biographical" truth about Boy.

This life-long professional hagiographer, even more frankly obsessed with biographical obligation than most other narrators of elegiac romance, makes up his own life out of writing "saints' lives," and in particular the double elegiac romance of his Shadow, Boy Staunton, and his Anima, Mrs. Dempster. Having explained these saints, these obsessively compelling persons of mythical import, he has explained himself out of his psychic entrapment by them. That he then goes on to further entrapment by Eisengrim and Liesl is part of another narrative pattern.

Davies has taken a vast amount from MacLennan, jokily re-shaped it into a Canadian Saint's Life, with the help of the legendary facts of the life of his narrator's namesake, St. Dunstan,[5] and refracted the result, I suspect, through the prism of Thomas Mann's ironic German Saint's Life, *Der Erwählte* (*The Holy Sinner,* 1954). *The Holy Sinner* was also "written" in St. Gall (a joint tribute to Jung?) by a celibate from abroad ("Clemens the Irishman"), while a guest at a very comfortable, care-free holy place, not unlike Davies' "Sorgenfrei"; it recounts the lives of ambiguously saintly figures much given to incest. The hero, a foundling, drifts ashore upon "St. Dunstan's Island"; a minor character is called *Eisen*grein and another *Grim*aldi; the hero, upon discovering his incest, abandons his mother-wife to her own penance, as she, Liesl-like, warns him against overdoing his; he spends seventeen years chained to a stone, which provides him milky nourishment; it is considerably larger than Dunstan's stone, but then Dunstan's penance—overdone, perhaps—is considerably longer. The analogy between Mann and Davies here may hint at some ironic refractions to Dunstan's saintliness and some further complications to Davies' intentions. Perhaps the Deptford-Zürich polarity may yield up literary as well as cultural-psychological allegories—a Mann-MacLennan dialectic, say, or, at the least, a deliberate "Canadianization" of Mann, in Davies' funny, ironic, compound saint's life.

Parallels at least as detailed could be drawn between Davies' *The Manticore*—in which a medical treatment at the top of a Swiss mountain turns into a hero-quest—and Mann's *The Magic Mountain*. In *World of Wonders*, of the several "Fausts" discussed, Mann's *Dr. Faustus* is pointedly missing. Davies, I think, is teasing us, as Liesl teases her auditors: "You surely know *Faust*? Not Goethe's *Faust*, of course; every Teuton has that by heart ... but the old German play on which he based his poem" (*WW*, 332).[6] "Not Marlowe's *Dr. Faustus*, but Thomas Mann's" might be the relevant "subtext" for us. Davies' artist-parable of the genius possessed by a daemon and counselled by a demon, with the egocentric moral obliquities and slurrings of feelings which are the drawbacks of those advantages, is of course less complex and subtle, and does not share the essential despair of Mann's ironic analysis of aesthetic profit and moral loss. Even to make the comparison is to stress the essentially parodic, even mock-heroic nature of Davies' relationship to Mann, or perhaps to suggest that the deeper affinities of *World of Wonders* are not with *Dr. Faustus*, but with *Felix Krull*. The young Hermes, the trickster-hero of the title, has some elegant affinities with the oft-disguised young Eisengrim; the latter's own "confessions" follow the Krullian pattern of an anti-Bildungsroman in the roguish-picaresque mode.

Felix Krull, to judge by Davies' frequent references in his essays (in which no modern author is mentioned oftener than Thomas Mann) is his favourite among Mann's texts, though both *Dr. Faustus* and *The Magic Mountain* are mentioned with respect and interest. Charmingly, a chief ground for Davies' approval of *Felix Krull* is that it is a fine, and astonishing, work for a writer already in his eighties. Could Mann be to Davies what Goethe was to Mann—the model, in both life and works, for being a distinguished author at a great age?

A touch of transcendence ends these books, as happens in many non-Canadian elegiac romances. The double experience of the narrator, lived through and then recaptured (retrouvé?) culminates in an epiphany of personal identity, secular, but with religious overtones, not without some moral portentousness, in the tremulous semi-Christian or semi-Jungian formulations of MacLennan and Davies, respectively.

Each book hints at an identity between narrator and hero: "Have I described Catherine? . . . Probably I have only described myself" (*WN*, 26) ; "Suddenly Jerome seemed to be inside me, *to be me*" (*WN*, 364) ; "It was as though [in visiting Mrs. Dempster] I were visiting a part of my own soul that was condemned to live in hell" (*FB*, 162). In *Fifth Business*, this identity even extends to include the author, in a kind of jokester's aesthetic epiphany that Davies might have picked up from Nabokov. Magnus Eisengrim=ME, DR= (approximately) the mirror-image of RD; that is to say, ME + DR=Robertson Davies. The epiphanies broaden out still further into identity with humanity and life at large ("Ah, Bartleby! Ah, humanity!" sighs Melville's narrator in the earliest of elegiac romances), acceptance of the gift of life and "the awful responsibility of Time" (as Jack Burden calls it at the end of *All the King's Men*), and, first and last, in all the elegiac romances, the ambiguous burden of self. "Be good to yourself," say Jerome and Liesl to their compulsive biographers. And, in the end, and in his own way, each narrator is. In his elegy to his "friend and enemy" (*FB*, 9), he has built his own monument.

UNIVERSITY OF BRITISH COLUMBIA

NOTES

¹ New York: Pantheon Books, 1973, to be referred to below as *MDR*.

² References to MacLennan and Davies (using the abbreviations *WN* and *FB*), will be given in the text, to the following editions: *The Watch That Ends the Night* (Toronto: Macmillan Co., 1975) ; *Fifth Business* (New York: New American Library, 1971).

³ I owe the term, the concept, and most of the salient features to Kenneth Bruffee, whose nearly-completed book-length manuscript and two articles, "Elegiac Romance," *College English* 32:4 (January 1971), 465-476, and "Nabokov's *Sebastian Knight*: An Example of Elegiac Romance," *Modern Language Quarterly* 34:2 (June 1973), 180-190, define and exemplify it further. At least thirteen Canadian titles could be added to his list of over sixty examples. See my forthcoming article, "The Biographical Compulsion: Elegiac Romances in Canadian Fiction," (*Journal of Modern Literature*, Spring, 1980), of which the present paper is a revised version of the first section, for fuller details on elegiac romance,

and particularly for a discussion of Robert Kroetsch's *The Studhorse Man* and A. M. Klein's *The Second Scroll* as elegiac romances. I thank the editor of *JML* for permission to reprint part of this article here.

4 "MacLennan's Rising Sun," (1959), in *Hugh MacLennan*, ed. Paul Goetsch, Critical Views on Canadian Writers (Toronto, 1973), pp. 119-22. Davies also admires the fusion of "storyteller" and "self-explorer" in George Stewart, while deploring the "vampirish" quality of Catherine's character. This article gains in significance for our present purposes, because Davies has written relatively little criticism of Canadian literature.

5 Wilfred Cude, "Miracle and Art in *Fifth Business*," *Journal of Canadian Studies* 9:4 (November 1974), 3-16.

6 *World of Wonders* (Toronto: Macmillan Co., 1975), p. 332. For further discussion of *WW* as Faustian and Gothic artist parable, see my article, "Neo-Modernism in the Canadian Artist-Parable: Hubert Aquin and Brian Moore," *Canadian Review of Comparative Literature* (Spring, 1979), esp. pp. 201-05.

The Great Mother and the Boy: Jung, Davies, and *Fifth Business*

F. L. Radford

When I am asked why I have spent so much time, over the past twenty-five years, in the study of the work and thought of Dr. C. G. Jung, I reply that it is because Jung's discoveries and speculations throw so much light on my work as a student and teacher of literature. Jung always insisted that he was a scientist, and unquestionably that was true; but he was also a great humanist, and although I deplore partial and facile application of Jungian ideas to literary criticism, I know that a serious study of Jungian thought is one fruitful path of literary study. (Robertson Davies)[1]

With its lucid surface and richly symbolic subsurface, *Fifth Business* gives us a representation of life as perceived by Jung, with its mundane and rational surface broken through at intervals by the symbols of myth and dream that express the hidden powers of the unconscious.[2] The happy thought of making the narrator an historian and hagiographer who believes in patterns of myth in history and the individual life frees the reader from the immediate demand for belief, since what he is shown may simply be Ramsay's way of seeing things and thus part of his character. Also, Ramsay comes to this way of seeing things from experiences in his life which the reader shares before being subjected to the theory. In this sense, the novel can be seen as educating the reader for the Jungian bias of the Deptford trilogy as a whole. In large measure, the Jungian pattern is centred on the theme of individuation typified in the myth of the Hero and the Mother, in which every obstacle on the ascendant path of the hero "wears the shadowy features of the Terrible Mother, who saps his strength with the poison of secret doubt" while every victory "wins back again the smiling, loving and life-giving mother."[3]

The first women to shape Ramsay's life are his own mother and Mary Dempster. In Jung's theory, the psychic power of the mother comes from "the archetype projected upon her, which gives her a mythological background and invests her with authority and numinosity."[4] The power of the archetype may be divided between the natural mother and a female figure who fills in something missing, as Mary Dempster does in Ramsay's psyche.

Ramsay's mother is the source of his crippling guilts. When her Scottish reserve breaks down in the dionysian frenzy of the beating over the stolen egg, he first knows the terror of uncontrolled possessiveness. When he submits to the ritual of pardon and is forgiven with a kiss, he is only more disturbed: "How could I reconcile this motherliness with the screeching fury who had pursued me around the kitchen with a whip, flogging me until she was gorged with—what? Vengeance? What was it? . . . But what I knew then was that nobody—not even my mother—was to be trusted in a strange world that showed very little of itself on the surface."[5] Here, surely, is the root of Ramsay's adult desire to find the myth behind reality. The anguish his mother provokes is matched only by two other experiences with women. The first is the destruction of his idealized vision of Faustina: "I have never known such a collapse of the spirit even in the worst of the war" (*FB*, 253). The second is the death of Mary Dempster, when the feelings repressed at his parents' deaths surge to the surface in "frightening dreams, in some of which my mother figured in terrible forms" (*FB*, 281). The latter confirms Mrs. Dempster's role as a partial mother substitute.

Davies keeps us aware that the human psyche cannot be defined by single images. Mrs. Ramsay may be a possessive demon-mother to her own son, but she is a saintly life-giver to Paul Dempster, whose mother cannot care for him because of the harm wrought by Staunton's stone in the snowball which caused Paul's premature birth. Ramsay later complains that his fellow soldiers cannot understand "that everyone has at least two, if not twenty-two, sides to him" when they will not see him as both the dourly religious "Deacon" and the profane "Chaplin" (*FB*, 78). He commits the same fault when he abstracts Mary Dempster into a Virgin Mother image. To the puritanical folk of Deptford her image is also one-sided: the minister's wife as whore, she embodies profane love at its worst. Led by Mrs. Ramsay, their hysterical reaction to her free action, in offering herself to a sex-starved tramp just because "he wanted it so badly" (*FB*, 50), follows exactly Freud's definition of the treatment of the taboo-breaker.[6] To her husband and son, Mary is the agent of undeserved guilt and punishment. To the Catholic priest, she is a "fool-saint" sent to lure Ramsay's unwary protestant soul to Hell—and thus an analogue of the Helen of Mephistopheles. Even Ramsay sees her for moments as other than a saint image: on the battlefield she appears as the sternly-judging "Crowned Woman" of *Revelation* and in her coffin she just looks "like a small, elderly woman, ready for burial" (*FB*, 282-83). Davies himself says of her, "My most recent work is a trilogy in which a madwoman is one of the central characters because, although she is demonstrably insane, her insanity releases trains of thought and feeling in other people which are immensely fruitful" (*OH*, 176).

The two women give Ramsay his initial models for responding to the world and its values. His own mother rules by dogma and follows the most conventional values of her society. Her definition of love is absolute loyalty, which gives her total possession of husband and sons (*FB*, 69). Mary Dempster lives "by a light that arose from within" (*FB*, 56). Even though her behaviour and the values it implies are abhorred by her society, and she is made an outcast, she remains at peace with herself. Ramsay's conservatism in later life comes from his mother; his insistence upon living by his own values, even though it costs him the Headmastership of his school, comes from Mary Dempster. But he thoroughly represses the image of Whore also associated with her in his psyche. Her sexual side does not easily accord with his idealization of her, so he decides "that this unknown aspect must be called madness" (*FB*, 57). His own mother increasingly assumes the aspect of the Terrible Mother, while he projects upon Mary Dempster the image of the Pièta which Jung opposes to the former.[7]

II

The war sequence climaxes in Ramsay's battlefield vision: lying wounded in the ruined church, he sees above him a statue of the Madonna of the Immaculate Conception. To him, it has the face of Mary Dempster and it is the "Crowned Woman" of *Revelation*. Davies is very accurate in his iconography, for in 1649 Pacheco, the inspector of sacred pictures for the Inquisition, laid down rules for the depiction of this Madonna: she was to be "clothed with the sun, having the moon under her feet, and on her head a crown of twelve stars"—the moon was to have its horns pointed downwards and under the Madonna's feet was also to be "the head of the bruised and vanquished dragon." The commentator points out that the idea is evidently "taken from the woman in the Apocalyse."[8] Jung argues that the Crowned Woman of *Revelation* is properly an *anima mundi* figure whose child should symbolize the reconciliation of opposites.[9] Instead, the child born, rather than the redeeming Christ, is one who will rule "with a rod of iron" (*Rev.* 12:5), so that we have an "enantiodromia"—the breaking through of the repressed opposite, an unforgiving Madonna and a punishing Christ. When this image combines with that of the Virgin, we have the punishing and comforting mother in a single icon. When we remember that Ramsay was driven to enlist while still two years underage by the intolerable conflict between his mother's demand for absolute loyalty and his devotion to Mary Dempster, it is not surprising that his psyche should transform the statue to fit his own personal cosmography.

Sinking into his coma, Ramsay corresponds to the hero visiting the underworld of the unconscious, which is symbolized in Jungian terms as the Mother: "The vision is apocalyptic: the mother-city in the land of eternal youth, surrounded by the flowery verdure of imperishable spring."[10] Ramsay feels "wonderfully at ease and healingly at peace" (FB, 85)—as he does not feel again until after the other great battle of the novel, his struggle and reconciliation with Liesl as the embodiment of the demonic in woman (FB, 262). In the meantime, like an Actaeon torn to pieces before seeing the goddess, his mutilation prepares him for his meeting with Diana Manners.

Diana indeed helps Ramsay to polish his manners and in another reversal of the Actaeon legend, she initiates him into sexual love. But, having revived him, fed and washed him, she also regards him "as her own creation" making him feel that she is "too much a mother" just at the point where he thinks he has been freed from the mother image by the death of his parents. He evades marriage to her because he has "no intention of being anybody's own dear laddie, ever again" (FB, 97). We must judge whether Ramsay is justified in his flight from Diana or is like that patient of Jung, who "always tried to evade his emotional needs. As a matter of fact he was afraid they might get him into trouble, for instance into marriage, and into other responsibilities such as love, devotion, loyalty, trust, emotional dependence and general submission to the soul's needs."[11]

In Jungian theory, Diana is a most complex symbolic figure. As the nymph of the spring of renewal, she is a "formulation of the figure we know as the anima." She is also "Luna, the 'mother of mortal bodies'" and is espoused to the "winged youth" who symbolizes "everything that is winged in the psyche or that would like to sprout wings" if it were not for the "poison of organizational thinking" and "the madness that sooner or later overtakes every mass—the death instinct of the lemmings. In the political sphere the name for this is war."[12] The other Diana, as Ramsay would have known from his childhood reading of the 1888 *Chambers' Encyclopedia*, was "Diana of the Ephesians" whose cult was an important variant of the worship of the Great Mother. Significantly, *Chambers'* points out that "she personified the fructifying powers of nature, . . . the attendants of her temple being eunuchs and women" (III, 458). Jung sees the elevation of the Holy Mother in the Catholic Church as the awakening of a necessary archetype of the human psyche, pointing out with glee that when "the Virgin Mary was declared the ΘΕΟΤΌΚΟΣ, 'birth-giver of the god'," in the year 431, it was "at the Council of Ephesus, whose streets had once rung with hymns of

69

praise to many-breasted Diana."[13] Diana was commonly shown as having "above her brow the crescent of the moon" (*Chambers'*, I, 458), while Ramsay's Madonna "stood on a crescent moon." In *The Golden Bough*, Diana is called "no other than the Queen of Heaven."[14] Ramsay's Diana is both the Pièta and the Terrible Mother. As nurse and comforter she is the former; perceived by his mother-ridden psyche as his new creatrix and would-be possessor, she is the latter.

III

Fleeing the dominion of the mother, Ramsay returns to Deptford to enact the role of public hero and confirm his escape from his childhood sweetheart, Leola, who marries Boy Staunton. He becomes a "good teacher" coaching "scores of boys privately for scholarships" without extra pay. He remarks, "As the years wore on I was finally acquitted of the suspicion that hangs over every bachelor schoolmaster—that he is homosexual, either overt or frying in some smoky flame of his own devising" (*FB*, 131). He becomes an historian fascinated by "the oddly recurring themes of history, which are also the themes of myth" (*FB*, 131). His values are conservative: "I don't regret economic and educational advance; I just wonder how much we shall have to pay for it, and in what coin" (*FB*, 228). He maintains a brotherly love-hate friendship with Boy Staunton and develops a close friendship with the rediscovered Paul Dempster. He tells us that he keeps up a lifelong friendship with Diana and his relationship with Liesl combines strong friendship with sexual love. He becomes a symbol of scholarly and aesthetic culture at Boy Staunton's parties. And already his battlefield vision has shown the receptivity to revelation which is to lead to his search for religious knowledge. When we take all this together, it is revealing to read Jung on the positive effects of a mother complex:

> Thus a man with a mother-complex may have a finely differentiated Eros instead of, or in addition to, homosexuality. . . . This gives him a great capacity for friendship, which often creates ties of astonishing tenderness between men and may even rescue friendship between the sexes from the limbo of the impossible. He may have good taste and an aesthetic sense which are fostered by the presence of a feminine streak. Then he may be supremely gifted as a teacher because of his almost feminine insight and tact. He is likely to have a feeling for history, and to be conservative in the best sense and cherish the values of the past. Often he is endowed with a wealth of religious feelings, which help to bring the *ecclesia spiritualis* into reality; and a spiritual receptivity which makes him responsive to revelation.[15]

As Ramsay is led towards the interest in saints that will make him a noted hagiographer, he finds that he is "rediscovering religion as well" (*FB*, 138). And the most detailed account we are given of his saint searches is of his visits to "every shrine" of the bearded virgin saint, Wilgefortis or Uncumber, to test his theory that her legend "might be a persistence of the hermaphrodite figure of the Great Mother" (*FB*, 162). This sounds like the conscious fascination with the thing that is feared on the unconscious level, which Jung describes as an effort "to sublimate fear into a desire for knowledge."[16] It is the effect of the "remnants of the child-soul in the adult":

> These archetypes . . . are the dominants that rule the pre-conscious soul of the child and, when projected upon the human parents, lend them a fascination which often assumes monstrous proportions. . . . Did the human father really possess this mysterious power, his sons would soon liquidate him or, even better, would refrain from becoming fathers themselves. For what ethical person could possibly bear so great a responsibility?[17]

For Ramsay, the monstrous figure is the mother, but for his counterpart, Paul Dempster, it is the father with his "extraordinary belief in guilt as an educative force" (*FB*, 301). It is also the father for David Staunton, in *The Manticore*. And all three "refrain from becoming fathers themselves."

Davies' use of myth to give psychic depth to his characters and Ramsay's matching awareness of myth behind the patterns of history and individual life recall the works of Joseph Campbell, whom Davies has called a "great scholar of the mythic world" (*OH*, 275). Campbell's synthesis of hero-myth, in *The Hero with a Thousand Faces*, gives much importance to sexual adjustment but, with Jungian complexity, the legends symbolic of the attainment of healthy sexual maturity are also seen to be symbolic of the healthy integration of the psyche as a whole. Thus, success in the test of "the loathly lady" can mean acceptance of both the fearsome side of woman and the fearsome side of life. In Campbell's view, the demonic side of the Great Mother "is at the root of such unattainable great goddess figures as that of the chaste and terrible Diana."[18] Her protecting side "appears in Christian saints' legends as the Virgin . . . and in Goethe's *Faust* successively as Gretchen, Helen of Troy, and the Virgin."[19] Ramsay's women also move between the protective and the demonic. He meets his Virgin, Gretchen and Helen of Troy in different order than Faust—in Mary Dempster, Leola and Faustina.

The Great Mother was Cybele, Goddess of the Moon, and great parent of gods and men. Recalling the flung stone which leads from the birth of Paul Dempster to the death of Boy Staunton, her sacred symbol was a small meteoric stone. She was Mother Nature, but her priests were eunuchs and her devotees practised self-emasculation in the delirium of worship. A bull was sacrificed to her in the *taurobolium*, but the alternate ceremony was the *criobolium*—the sacrifice of a ram, recalling Ramsay on the battlefield. As Diana, the inscription on her temple was "Know thyself." Jung points out that the philosopher's stone, in alchemical symbolism, was "the mother of that which is made" and that "the secret nature of the stone was man's own self."[20] When Boy Staunton is faced with the stone from the snowball, at the end of *Fifth Business*, it is as an emblem of his true self: "The stone-in-the-snowball has been characteristic of too much you've done for you to forget it forever!" (*FB*, 305). But it is Ramsay who carries the stone with him all his life, and one of the few things he mentions noticing on his return home to take inventory after his parents' deaths is the stone that his father "had brought from Dumfries and always used as a paperweight" (*FB*, 115).

As Ramsay's account of Wilgefortis suggests, there was generally an hermaphroditic aspect to the Great Mother figures. Cybele was accompanied by Attis—an emasculated male—as Ramsay's father is the emasculated consort of his mother in the rites of their home. Jung mentions that Attis was known as "the Lord of the sacred Ram."[21] Ramsay's father devised the pledge made to his mother after the stolen egg incident: "that I would always love my mother, to whom I owed the great gift of life, and that I begged her—and secondarily God—to forgive me" (*FB*, 36). After his mother's death, Ramsay says, "I knew she had eaten my father and I was glad I did not have to fight any longer to keep her from eating me" (*FB*, 89). In fleeing Diana Manners, Ramsay believes he is escaping a similar fate. In his explanation of the Crowned Woman, Jung describes the "elect" of *Revelation* in a way that suggests Ramsay's escape is merely a variation of the same fate. They follow "the young dying god" and "have never become complete human beings, but have voluntarily renounced their share in the human lot and have said no to the continuance of life on earth." As "the male virgins, 'which are not defiled with women'" they "really belong to the cult of the Great Mother ... like the priests of Cybele who used to castrate themselves in honour of her son Attis."[22] Although Ramsay is no virgin in the literal sense, much of the rest of this can be applied to him, and the loss of his leg can readily be seen as a displaced castration. It is notable that in their great comic battle in the bedroom, Liesl uses his wooden leg as a weapon in her effort to subdue him (*FB*, 256). Liesl has an androgynous aspect and when the Great Mother comes to demand payment from Boy Staunton, it is as Denyse Hornick who, according to Staunton's threadbare stereotypes, has a "masculine mind" (*FB*, 270).

72

Denyse's first name recalls Dionysus, a god of androgynous aspect, whose incarnation as a bull was worshipped by female devotees wearing horns[23]— echoed by her last name. Jung says that the "terrible mother" is also "represented by the most paradoxical god of the Greek pantheon, Dionysus" and in this form "drives the son to madness and self-mutilation." Jung adds, "As a primal being the mother represents the unconscious."[24] When Denyse says that Ramsay must write Boy's "official life" she speaks "like a mother" and her demand is "not so much an inquiry as a flick of the whip" (*FB*, 292)— recalling the whip with which Mrs. Ramsay fixed in her son's mind the image of the Terrible Mother (*FB*, 35-36). But Ramsay himself also partakes of the Dionysus image: he is dismembered and "dies" on the battle-field in November; is "born again" in May; and is rechristened by Diana at Christmas, by the pouring of wine on his head—and he contributes to Boy Staunton's destruction. Ramsay's *Chambers' Encyclopedia* would have told him that Dionysus was called the "twice born."

Ramsay shares the juvenile influence of Leola only with Boy Staunton, but he shares crucial female influences with Paul Dempster. His own demon-mother has been for a time a saintly foster-mother to Paul. Faustina is a useful stage *symbol* of the feminine for Dempster, as Magnus Eisengrim, but an angelic and demonic *embodiment* of the feminine for Ramsay. For both, Liesl is a demonic guide who becomes benign when courageously overcome and embraced. But each one of the three has his own first initiation to sexual experience and it largely shapes his future character. For Boy Staunton, it is loveless fumbling with the pathetic Mabel Heighington and he stays at the juvenile level of a Don Juan. For Paul Dempster, it is rape as a masturbatory object by Willard the Wizard and he becomes confined to his own ego, "his compelling love affair" being "with himself" (*FB*, 252). For Ramsay, it is the mutually fulfilling affair with Diana Manners, shadowed by his obsession with the demon-mother, but ending in mature friendship. He remains the only one capable of true giving and receiving with a woman, although he denies himself this fulfillment until it is almost too late for its life-giving powers to have effect. Much of all this is prefigured in the responses of the three to Mary Dempster's "sin." For the young Boy Staunton it merely gives the opportunity to identify woman as "whoor"; for Paul Dempster it is seen only as a source of pain for himself; for Ramsay it is the source of commitment to the woman herself, against popular opinion, enabling him finally to perceive the sinner as a saint.

Ramsay's particular offence against the Great Mother is to deny wholeness to women: his "saint" is no more allowed full humanity than Staunton's "whoor." Divided into saints, demons, or nonentities, women acquire individuality and importance for him only when they bring to the surface the fear and desire associated with the mother image. It is only after he passes the test of "the loathly lady" in meeting, fighting and embracing Liesl that he is able to reconcile the demonic and angelic sides of the *Magna Mater* and accept woman as a whole being.

Jung's concepts of the Anima and the Shadow are used with proper complexity by Davies. Jung argues that the Shadow, as a symbol of the "primitive" in the human psyche, can have positive forces of natural instinct and spontaneity. Similarly, the Anima as a projection of the male soul into a female image is not merely angelic but a force urging the psyche towards self-knowledge and wholeness. As such it can have strong demonic elements and when Ramsay projects a devil image unto Liesl that does not make her an embodiment of the Shadow in his psyche. Davies himself has called her "a fierce witch,"[25] but in discussing Byron's *Manfred* he has referred to "the Witch of the Alps, a figure of the dark side of the Anima, whom one is sometimes inclined to think might have been a better match for Manfred than the beautiful Astarte" (*OH*, 150). Liesl's home, of course, is in the Swiss Alps. As a reflection of Ramsay, even Liesl's grotesque features suggest an exaggeration of his own "scowling and cadaverous cast of countenance" (*FB*, 121). She is a "loathly lady" figure who can also show "captivating intellect and charm" (*FB*, 240). After attacking with ruthless physical violence, she gives Ramsay the greatest sexual pleasure of his life. She is the unifying figure between him and Eisengrim: a female of male appearance, she unites the two men's sexual worlds; a scholar who is skilled in the practical mechanics of stage illusion, she unites their professional worlds; and it is she who invites Ramsay backstage in Mexico and renews their childhood relationship. Then Ramsay taught Paul Dempster about magic and read him legends of the saints; now Ramsay advises Eisengrim on the subjects of his illusions and transmutes the saints' legends into the Romance of Magnus Eisengrim.

Before offering Ramsay advice, Liesl pointedly denies that she is "an English lady, or somebody's mother" (*FB*, 253), but in Ramsay's personal mythology she is Caredwen, the demonic mother goddess of the Celts (*FB*, 133). The "aftermath of healing tenderness" (*FB*, 262) she brings strongly recalls the promise of Campbell's benign Cosmic Mother "that the peace of Paradise, which was known first within the mother womb, is not to be lost; that it supports the present and stands in the future as well as in the past."[26] The mother as the guardian of paradise appears again when Eisengrim accuses Staunton of being in debt to him "for eighty days in Paradise" for having caused his premature birth (*FB*, 306). Staunton is the only one of the three who never meets Liesl and if he did he would surely be unable to see past her forbidding exterior. It is clear that Denyse Hornick is for Staunton what Liesl is for Ramsay: what Jung calls "the demon-woman of mythology" who "is in truth the 'sister-wife-mother,' the woman in the man, who unexpectedly turns up during the second half of life and tries to effect a forcible change of personality." The response can be a "fossilization of the man" with "feelings of distrust and resentment"—Boy Staunton in the last part of *Fifth Business*—or the acquisition of energy for the "heroic conflict" that completes the "individuation process" where "the mother-symbol no longer connects back to the beginnings, but points towards the unconscious as the creative matrix of the future." The resulting wholeness consists of "a tremendous tension of opposites paradoxically at one with themselves."[27]

Ramsay has been publicly anointed hero long ago, in London and Dept-ford. When he describes his battle and reconciliation with Liesl he is privately anointed hero by Padre Blazon: "You met the Devil as an equal, not cringing or frightened or begging for a trashy favour. That is the heroic life, Ramezay. You are fit to be the Devil's friend without any fear of losing yourself to Him!" (*FB*, 288). In confirming Mary Dempster's heroism in the same conversation. Blazon also seems to exclude Eisengrim from the hero role: "Heroism in God's cause is the mark of the saint, Ramezay, not con-juring tricks" (*FB*, 287). It is immediately after this that Ramsay rediscovers his Little Madonna of Passchendaele and finds that she has "lost her sceptre" (*FB*, 290). It appears that the struggle with the Great Mother has been won at last.

IV

It has been argued that the novel should end with Ramsay's apparent achievement of his "authentic" self,[28] but this would be to impose an existentialist solution upon a work that is essentially Jungian in shape. An existentialist may believe that a permanently "authentic" self can be main-tained but Jung argues that it is the struggle for integration of the warring aspects of the psyche that is permanent—that the "hero's victory over the 'mother' or over her daemonic representative (dragon, etc.), is never any-thing but temporary."[29] Ramsay's crippling duality towards women has been resolved but he retains "two, if not twenty-two, sides to him" (*FB*, 78). The same guide who has cured his obsession with the possessive demon-mother has also given him the "Fifth Business" identity that enables him to rationa-lize his betrayal of Staunton: "Here it was. Either I spoke now or I kept silence forever. Dunstan Ramsay counselled against revelation, but Fifth Business would not hear" (*FB*, 304). At the end of *World of Wonders* Ramsay is still obsessed with Boy Staunton's death and still evading his own responsibility. He warns us himself that "the beginning and end of the conjurer's art" is "that subtle technique of misdirecting the attention of his audience" (*FB*, 242). It is not only Eisengrim who practices this art, but Staunton hiding his ruthless power-hunger behind the image of "Boy" and his huge financial holdings behind the unimposing facade of "Alpha Corporation" (*FB*, 169)—and Ramsay hiding his roles of hero and villain behind that of Fifth Business. Padre Blazon points out what is obvious, that there is nothing in this concept that belongs uniquely to Ramsay: "we all bring ill-luck to others, you know, often without in the least recognizing it" (*FB*, 285-86). Davies himself says of his three central characters, "Any of the three is a man whom we might like, or detest, if we met him casually. All three are, in various ways, liars. All three do some good in the world and some evil. But it is in the inner life that one is almost a saint, one a failure, and one a hero" (*OH*, 17).

Ramsay's demonic side is closely tied to the far-reaching effects of Staunton's stone-in-the-snowball and is largely expressed in relation to Boy and women. Ramsay sneers at Staunton's sterile love affairs and claims that he himself "never used a woman simply as an object" (*FB*, 132) but he makes his women into the anonymous jokes, Agnes Day, Gloria Mundy and Libby Doe. When he tells us that Staunton thinks Denyse has a "masculine mind" because she can understand his ideas, we may remember that Ramsay thinks women lack sufficient humour to enjoy the funny side of sex with "a one-legged philanderer" (*FB*, 133) and that he shares the old view that an education designed for men does some kind of indistinct psychic harm to women. When he finds that Leola has left a suicide note that could compromise him, he is outraged, but we recall that he has tacitly encouraged her belief that he has remained single because of love for her so that her despair was intensified when he rejected her after she had been rejected by Staunton. Ramsay specializes in this kind of concealed revenge on all of those who cause him guilt or envy. He even punishes his mother, before he learns of her death, by withholding news of his survival and his medal. When he turns Mary Dempster from "a woman who was simple and nothing worse" into one who must be kept "in the wing where the windows are barred" (*FB*, 268), he tells us twice that his action was the result of "stupidity"—but he has known for a long time that any mention of her son is deeply disturbing. We have been told earlier of the demented Athelstan woman who dislikes Ramsay because he seems to "remind her of some false

76

friend in the past" (*FB*, 13). Now the demented Mary Dempster thinks of him "as the evil genius of her life" (*FB*, 280). This may be unfair, but he has in some sense exploited her for the needs of his own psyche. When he visits her in the mental hospital he describes it as being "as though I were visiting a part of my own soul that was condemned to live in hell" (*FB*, 206). Ramsay's projection of parts of his own psyche onto others is not without cost to them.

Ramsay shares characteristics that he criticizes in others. His vaunted integrity is compromised early in accepting Staunton's financial advice as a kind of unacknowledged bribe for silence. When he tells Boy that the stone-in-the-snowball secret must be revealed because it has been characteristic of Staunton's whole life, we remember that Ramsay has kept the actual stone at the core of his life—apparently waiting for the strategic moment of revenge.

The sacrificial stance favoured by Ramsay is always two-sided and the dual significance of the icon on the battlefield is symbolic of his psyche in this. As the Madonna it is the forgiving and comforting Anima; as the Crowned Woman it is the primitive and vengeful Shadow. Jung argues that the John of *Revelation* releases the repressed anger of the John of the *Epistles*. In *Revelation* the Book is opened by a horned Lamb, which is "more like a ram than a lamb ... the aggressive and irascible ram whose rage can at last be vented." It is "the outburst of long pent-up negative feelings such as can frequently be observed in people who strive for perfection."[30] In caring for Mary Dempster, Ramsay is conscious that he is sacrificing himself for the sins of Boy Staunton. But he will not give Staunton a chance to absolve himself by helping: "I was determined that if I could not take care of Mrs. Dempster, nobody else should do it. She was mine" (*FB*, 206). He does not see that he may be using Mary Dempster to expiate his abandonment of his own mother, but he has terrible dreams of the latter on the night of Mary Dempster's death. And Staunton is finally required to pay for the forgotten sin that has cost Ramsay so much.

It is true that Staunton must face the reality of his own Shadow if he is to recover from the spiritual accidie that afflicts the last part of his life, but in defining the guilt of another Ramsay is evading his own responsibilities. In Jungian terms, it is more valuable to know and accept one's own guilt, "because it is a part of one's own self," than to "project one's shadow on to others."[31] The necessary counterpart is to be reconciled with the evil in oneself: "Christ espoused the sinner and did not condemn him. . . . And as little as we would accuse Christ of fraternizing with evil, so little should we reproach ourselves that to love the sinner who is oneself is to make a pact

77

with the devil."[32] It is these two Jungian precepts that Liesl tries to reconcile for Ramsay.

She points out the real failures in his life, saying, "That horrid village and your hateful Scots family made you a moral monster" and calling his agonized and comic infatuation with Faustina "the revenge of the unlived life" (FB, 250, 260). Davies has described the latter as the sacrifice of love for "a career, or an idea of one's place in the world, or simply . . . to serve one's own comfort and egotism" (OH, 239). One could argue that Eisengrim does the first, Staunton the second, and Ramsay the third. Davies argues that Evil is frequently "depicted as the failure of Love, or to use the older word that has no merely romantic overtone, of loving kindness" (OH, 263). Liesl also repeats the earlier advice of Padre Blazon: "Forgive yourself for being a human creature, Ramezay. That is the beginning of wisdom" (FB, 204, 259). By the end of the novel, which is the start of his "report" to the Headmaster, Ramsay is still hiding from full self-knowledge in "the vital though never glorious role of Fifth Business" (FB, 10), but he has succeeded in recovering the personal archetypes he had projected upon his mother and Mary Dempster. In his true role as Jung's hero of the psyche, his journey begins with flight from the demon-mother and ends with the "healing tenderness" of the embrace of the demon-mistress. To this extent he has succeeded in the self-healing Jung describes as follows:

> An archetype as such is in no sense just an annoying prejudice: it becomes so only when it is in the wrong place. In themselves, archetypal images are among the highest values of the human psyche; they have peopled the heavens of all races from time immemorial. To discard them as valueless would be a distinct loss. Our task is not, therefore, to deny the archetype, but to dissolve the projections, in order to restore their contents to the individual who has involuntarily lost them by projecting them outside himself.[33]

Presumably this recovery has taken place when Ramsay is able to say of the rediscovered Madonna statue, "I needed no picture. She was mine forever" (FB, 290).

Ramsay is less disastrously trapped in his own ego than either Staunton or Eisengrim and their one-sidedness gives us a more accurate measure for him. His possessiveness of Mary Dempster as a symbolic abstraction is destructive, but he does care for her at some cost to himself both as child and adult. He has a soured view of the nature of boys, but he does give valuable time to tutoring without pay. As a scholar he follows what he considers important at the cost of preferment in his profession. He passes through the stages of life more successfully than the others and achieves a greater measure of psychic growth. He survives "the revenge of the unlived life" which destroys Staunton and is evaded by Eisengrim. When Davies sets the sensational danger and suffering of the battlefield against the danger and suffering of the psyche in everyday life, it is Ramsay who experiences them both most fully and who shows us that the latter are as intense and important as the former. He stands enough above the other two to be a representative hero-figure with a message for those who follow. The novel is his "report" to the Headmaster, the one responsible for the education of future generations. More than a reply to Packer's patronizing eulogy of Ramsay in the school paper, it is a warning of the cost of a Deptford childhood in terms of belated acceptance of one's own humanity and that of others. The crippling effects of what Eisengrim calls "an extraordinary belief in guilt as an educative force" (*FB*, 301) can never be wholly cured any more than Ramsay's artificial leg wholly replaces his real one.

It is a fine touch that Davies brings back unacknowledged guilt on the last page of *Fifth Business*: a more "authentic" conclusion than any neat resolution of all contradictions. Of those the Brazen Head accuses of contributing to Staunton's suicide, only Ramsay is clearly identified: "the inevitable fifth, who was keeper of his conscience and keeper of the stone" (*FB*, 308). The resulting heart seizure allows Ramsay both to expiate his responsibility for Staunton's death and to evade direct acknowledgement of his own guilt—just as his sacrifice on the battlefield did for his mother-conflict. This ending leaves the reader room for creative speculation and leaves the character of Ramsay humanly alive, with room for the growth and self-understanding that should only end with death. It also saves Davies from the accusation that he commits the sin he ascribes to Dickens' Fagin: that "he makes evil appear to be good" (*OH*, 214). Davies perceives a two-fold concept of evil in Jungian thought. There is an evil in the self which must be acknowledged and reconciled with good, to prevent its projection unto others and to "produce a new and stronger spirit in man" which "appears in the form of a wider sensibility, a greater wisdom, and an enlarged charity" (*OH*, 263). But there is also "a power of good and a power of evil external to man, and working through him as an agency—a God, in fact, infinitely greater than man can conceive, and a Devil vastly more terrible than even the uttermost terrors of human evil" (*OH*, 264). It is clear that Ramsay's Mary Dempster and Liselotte Vitzlipützli, as Saint and Devil, belong to the former realm rather than the latter. The vision of unmotivated evil that David Staunton glimpses incarnate in Bill Unsworth, in the vandalism scene of *The Manticore*, defines the difference.[34] The external power of Evil is also seen in the "murky, fiery light" of the flames burning the Kaiser's effigy in Deptford, as Ramsay sees his "own people" delighting "in a symbolic act of cruelty and hatred" (*FB*, 114). Ramsay is a character who achieves in considerable measure the wholeness of the psyche to be gained from the "new and stronger spirit" and our understanding of the close links between his characterization and Jung's concepts of individuation and integration of the psyche helps us to judge how far he has come and how far he has still to go.

UNIVERSITY OF ALBERTA

NOTES

[1] *One Half of Robertson Davies* (Toronto: Macmillan, 1977), p. 143. The many future references to this work will be identified by initials and page number, thus: (*OH*, 143).

[2] Davies has said that his Deptford novels "are written in a fashion that makes them seem to be simpler than in fact they are" (*OH*, 16-17).

[3] C. G. Jung, *Symbols of Transformation* in *Collected Works* (Princeton: University Press, 1970), V, 389-90.

[4] C. G. Jung, "Psychological Aspects of the Mother Archetype," in *Basic Writings* (New York: Modern Library, 1959), p. 335.

[5] Robertson Davies, *Fifth Business* (New York: Viking, 1970). Future references to this novel will be identified thus: (*FB*, 89).

[6] Sigmund Freud, "Totem and Taboo," trans. James Strachey, in *Complete Psychological Works* (London, 1955), XIII, 32. A popular moral history regularly reprinted from the 1870's to the 1920's expresses the case in terms that would be more acceptable to the ladies of Deptford:

> Here, then, the abhorrence of the impure, the sense of duty, the fear of punishment, all unite and form a moral law which women themselves enforce, becoming the guardians of their own honour, and treating as a traitor to her sex the woman who betrays her trust. . . . It is forbidden to receive her; it is an insult to women to allude to her existence, to pronounce her name. She is condemned without inquiry, as the officer is condemned who has shown cowardice before the foe. For the life of women is a battle-field: virtue is their courage, and peace of mind is their reward.

(Winwoode Reade, *The Martyrdom of Man*. London, 1875, pp. 456-57).

[7] *Collected Works*, V, 425.

[8] Anna Brownell Jameson, *Legends of the Madonna as Represented in the Fine Arts* (London: Unit Library, 1903), p. 131.

[9] *Collected Works*, XI, 438-43.

[10] *Collected Works*, V, 411.

[11] *Collected Works*, XI, 506.

[12] *Mysterium Conjunctionis* in *Collected Works* (London: Routledge & Kegan Paul, 1963), XIV, 163-65.

[13] *Collected Works*, XI, 129; see also 312.

[14] Sir James Frazer, *The Golden Bough*, abridged edition (New York: Macmillan, 1951), p. 823.

[15] *Basic Writings*, pp. 337-38.

[16] *The Development of Personality* in *Collected Works* (London: Routledge & Kegan Paul, 1954), XVII, 17.

[17] *Collected Works*, XVIII, 45-46.

[18] *The Hero With a Thousand Faces* (1949; rpt. New York: World Publishing, 1956), p. 111.

[19] *Hero*, p. 71.

[20] *Collected Works*, XI, 94-98.

[21] *Aion* in *Collected Works*, IX (Princeton: University Press, 1968), 89n.

[22] *Collected Works*, XI, 445.

[23] *Collected Works*, V, 57n.

[24] *Collected Works*, V, 401 and 424.

[25] Radio interview on "Sunday Supplement," CBC Radio, October 19, 1975.

[26] *Hero*, pp. 71-72.

[27] *Collected Works*, V, 300-03. At this point, Jung is describing the case of a woman for whom the activating image was a male, Animus, figure. Presumably, in a different novel, Ramsay might be the "demon-man" for Liesl's psyche: as Giles Revelstoke is for Monica Gall in Davies' *A Mixture of Frailties*.

[28] David M. Monaghan, "Metaphors and Confusions," *Can. Lit.*, 69 (Winter, 1976), 64-73.

[29] *Collected Works*, V, 301.

[30] *Collected Works*, XI, 435-38.

[31] *Collected Works*, XIV, 168.

[32] *Psychology and Alchemy* in *Collected Works* (London: Routledge & Kegan Paul, 1953), XII, 31-32.

[33] *Basic Writings*, p. 336.

[34] *The Manticore* (Toronto: Macmillan, 1972), pp. 151 and 225.

The Manticore and the Law

Peter Brigg

It is a cliché that each man sees the world through his profession, but conventional wisdom usually stops at such external aspects as doctors seeing everyone as a patient or cooks seeing everyone as a stomach to be filled. The obvious and often comic aspects of these truisms tend to obscure the very deep truth that professional perspective ranks second only to familial nurture in the foundation of one's world view. In his complex portrayal of David Staunton's associations with the law in *The Manticore*, Robertson Davies undertakes to expand in depth how David's perception is conditioned by his loyalty to the law. David, as narrator, appears to present a thorough, factual account of his life and tribulations, a life of which a distinguished criminal lawyer would be proud. But he discovers he is in the hands of an equally distinguished advocate whose own expertise is in an area of human life beyond the codes on which his life is constructed, and in Johanna von Haller's special "court" David's evidence takes on a quality of very shaky pleading. David's narration continually reinforces the legal framework of his point of view but the outcome of the novel involves an expansion of his perspectives and an understanding of the law in a larger context.

This study will pose and attempt to answer a series of questions in order to investigate *The Manticore* and the law. It will consider why David followed the law and who influenced him in his understanding of it. It will examine just how the law actually affects David in the novel, including its effects on the narrative voice. It will study the forces which act to modify David's view of the world and will conclude by proposing several broader meanings for this particular fable of identity.

David himself offers a single, powerful explanation for his pursuit of the law: the incident to which he is party, along with two other boys and ringleader Bill Unsworth. When the boys break up and crudely defile a Muskoka summer cottage, David realizes, while actually watching Unsworth defecate upon the owners' family photographs, that he wishes to oppose people who act in this fashion. This initially appears to be a clear and rational decision, but closer examination shows that the incident only crystallizes David's deeply seated feelings about acts of this sort. He dismisses motives such as revenge or envy for Unsworth's act and is left with a conclusion surprising for someone whose profession requires a powerful exercise of materialistic reason: "... —he [Unsworth] is simply being as evil as his strong will and deficient imagination will permit. He is possessed, and what possesses him is Evil."[1] The reference to "Evil" obviously comes from a system of values David already holds, and it is necessary to turn to some aspects of his first sixteen years to divine the sources of David's moral decision to follow the law.

Nature's contribution to David's personality is difficult to gauge beyond his obvious inheritance of energetic self-confidence from his father and grandfather. From the retrospective position of his narrative, David himself suggests that he always possessed a strong sense of reason: "But I seem to have been born with an unusual regard for authority and the power of reason ... " (pp. 90-91), and this is clearly reinforced in his recollection of certain experiences.

> I was told I was fortunate. Indeed, Netty insisted that I thank God for it every night, on my knees. I believed it, but I wondered why I was thanking God when it was so obviously my father who was the giver of all good things. (p. 82)

However, it is in the area of nurture, of David's upbringing and experiences, that his desire to follow the law can be seen to be formed.

At the root of David's moral view lies the relationship with his father, who formed David's life in a fashion at once arbitrary and accidental. David begins his Zürich notebook by demonstrating how his father held him in an almost unconscious captivity by regulating his supply of money. Dr. von Haller and the reader quickly see that Boy Staunton's planned sexual initiation of David by Myrrha Martindale is the cause of David's celibacy for the twenty-three years between the event and his analysis. The power of David's reaction to this situation reveals how deeply offended he was at being at his father's mercy and how fiercely David's psyche fought back by his depriving Boy of the grandson he so desired. Despite the surface impression that David hero-worships his father there is no doubt that he is frequently forced to submerge his sense of reason and fairness in the face of Boy's anarchic, driven deeds and twisted legalism. In Dr. von Haller's consulting room this paradox surfaces frequently. We see examples in Boy's mistreatment of Leola, in Boy's arbitrary and clichéd refusals of David's requests for money until the sudden breakthrough when Boy is amused by David's love affair with Judith Wolff, and in the rules Boy arbitrarily lays down:

> I am sure he [Boy] was right, and I have always wished I could live
> according to his advice. I have never managed it. Nor did he, as I gradu-
> ally became aware, but somehow that was different. (p. 82)

Boy's final judgment on David (although it occurs after David chooses the
law) is the legal judgment of the will, the *damnosa hereditas* for failing to
do what Boy wished. Boy Staunton is always David's judge and always seeks
to make his son as much like himself as possible. David's reaction to being
judged and governed by a most irrational and capricious father is to seek the
heights of the great stone mountain of the tablets of law and precedence,
where he can exist in the clear air of reason, formality, and tradition, free
of the mists of paternal emotion and caprice. David claims to have seen this
situation when he went to Oxford, for he gives as part reason for his choice
a description of his father that could just as well be applied to Bill Unsworth:

> I wanted to get away from Father and save my soul, insofar as I
> believed in such a thing. I suppose what I meant by my soul was my self-
> respect or my manhood.... He too was a manipulator and, remembering
> his own dictum, I did not mean to be a man who could be manipulated.
> (p. 223)

This powerful desire to escape from the judgment of human subjectivity
and irrational caprice confronts David again and again as his personality is
being formed. As a tiny boy he encounters Grandfather Staunton's irrational
campaign against constipation with its purgatives and the enema device,
Dr. Tyrrell's Domestic Internal Bath. The obvious Freudian symbolism of
anal fixation is glossed over in the novel, but it is a characteristic formative
aspect of a logical, orderly personality. More importantly, David vividly
remembers attempting to apply logic to the situation by asking his grandfather whether he himself used the Internal Bath. The apparent failure of
this attempt resulted from an inability to cross-question so powerful a figure
of authority, and as a criminal lawyer David was later to be able to subject
even the mighty to real tests of the truth of evidence.

Other potent forces of injustice or irrationality in David's youth include
Netty Quelch, his sister Caroline, Father Knopwood, and Dr. Wolff. Netty
is a personification of Ontario Calvinism with her powerful devotion to
work, her elevation of Duty, her enclosed and unrealized personal life
(including her unspoken but vividly demonstrated love for Boy), and her
fund of clichés to be used in place of knowledge or information. Her judgment of Leola, horribly coloured by her passion for Boy, is so absolute in its
subjectivity that there is a possibility it leads to murder. Netty is so completely in the "right" as a dutiful servant that she encloses David's childhood

in a cocoon of unarguable dominance, often making it a hell from which he longs to escape into independence. Caroline confronts David with her skill as a manipulator of emotions, and, whether she is teasing and embarrassing him about Judith Wolff, drawing Netty's fangs at the managed dinner party, or planting in David the suspicion that he is not his father's son, she is a confusing illustration to him of those who fall victim to the untamable forces of human emotion. David's response to this disconcerting power is to seek the arena where the emotions are curbed or punished, the courtroom. In Father Knopwood David encounters a very different sort of force, for Knopwood is a man of iron will and a penetrating intelligence. He leads David to use his intelligence on the subject of art, to perceive that accepted wisdom is not to be trusted but that the mind must seek out real truth for itself. He also offers David a solid and attractively logical presentation of dogma and with it a clear series of moral precepts:

> I liked dogma, for the same reason that I grew to like law. It made sense, it told you where you stood, and it had been tested by long precedent. (p. 152)

But Knopwood's largely positive influence on David founders when Knopwood judges Boy's behaviour. David's violent reaction illustrates the depth of his attraction to Knopwood's proffered system and awakes David to the injustices that accompany the assumption of crusading moral superiority. It is a form of that superiority which David encounters in the Wolffs, for their civilized natures conceal a mixture of cultural snobbery and irrational racial prejudice that dooms his love for Judith. In his affair with Judy, David is victim of the irrational injustice of the structures beneath the veil of society. His sensitive intellect forces him to conclude, from his relationships with all of the important people in his youth, that he must free himself from situations where he is mastered by injustices and the subjective whims of others in order to establish a place from which he can command the baffling array of variables that affect his life. His solution, of course, is to read law and to go into the courtroom where the Bill Unsworths of the world are brought within the control of a rational and orderly tradition. The "Evil" against which David sets himself is the sum of human irrationality.

Once he has chosen the law David develops a complex view of it, one which will be seen to extend its influence far beyond the courtroom into every facet of his life. His first and greatest teacher is Pargetter, the Balliol don who supervises his formal studies and who, as his "father in art," is undoubtedly one of "the fathers you can choose for yourself" whom Ramsay later mentions to David. Davies draws a powerful and simple portrait of Pargetter which can be seen as a series of images for the law as David grasps it. Pargetter's passion for chess is sharply symbolic of an intelligence that wishes—in contrast with the five-leveled chessboard of Liesl and Eisengrim —to play within a fixed, invariable context. Pargetter encourages David to learn by bookish precedent not only the law itself but human nature as well, urging him to read the great novelists, historians and philosophers rather than to study clients. David even learns legal oratory from past speeches, a traditional approach which contributes to an image of the law virtually devoid of living humanity. Pargetter, the blind don, is a bachelor who actually advises David to "put your emotions in cold storage" in order to devote at least his youth to the law. Although he frequently and reasonably warns David against trying to master the law completely or falling into the trap of excessively romanticizing it, he himself appears to David—as they sit together in Pargetter's darkened rooms playing chess or discussing law— as a romantic master of the craft. In a very real sense Pargetter's life is the law, which later causes David to express his shock that Pargetter left no will, thus revealing a human weakness behind the mask of complete devotion to a world pictured through legal strictures.

Lest it should appear that Pargetter's influence upon David was wholly negative, credit must be given him for sharpening David's powers of reasoning and logic and for teaching him his profession superbly. In the cool, reasonable climate of Oxford David finds a haven from the forces that have manipulated him and realizes that with the law as his mistress there will be no emotional midnight scenes and no sudden and apparently unmotivated changes in the rules of the game. He speaks of the training in such a way that the reader realizes it is to be the substitute for meeting and handling the emotional within himself: "Exactitude, calm appraisal, close reasoning applied to problems which so often had their beginning in other people's untidy emotions acted like balm on my hurt mind" (p. 225). The cool attractiveness of this proposition hides the dangerous refusal to see that "untidy emotions" may have powers and effects beyond the rule of law and that it is not possible to force all of human reality into Pargetter's tidy, carefully annotated law library.

David removes himself from the British temples of the law to enter Canadian practice in rural Pittstown where his experience also influences his view of the law. There Diarmuid Mahaffey, a clever though less powerfully concentrated lawyer, both teaches David about human nature and gives him cases which teach him notable lessons. David learns a practical truth, one that Pargetter's stress on reading the humanities could never have taught, when one of his early clients, a Maltese labourer, solemnly denies having attempted a rape. When he is sentenced, and admits his guilt to David, David realizes how difficult it will always be to trust the many clients he will be dealing with. His next client, a murderess, teaches David different lessons, first about the need to probe for unvolunteered information about "people's untidy emotions" and second about the value of playing upon the emotions of judge and jury.

With the hanging of Jimmy Veale David finds his confidence in the edifice of the law severely tested, for it brings home to him the sordid face that justice may put on. He is left considering the besmirching demands society places on the law and painfully aware that he has chosen as a career the role of "Devil's Advocate" for the very "Evil" which he entered the law to oppose. The rationalization he accepts, that every man, guilty or not, must have his chance, leads him to create for himself an image of disinterested cunning, of a player who will take either black or white pieces in the game of the law.

Influencing David's attitude to the law less directly is a reflection of that rural Calvinist Ontario Consciousness which surrounds him throughout his life, even when he practices in the overgrown rural town of Toronto. He sees the law as the extension of the will of a community where authority figures, be they "Doc" Staunton, Boy Staunton or Netty Quelch, issue a stiff and unrelenting call for duty, order, obedience, and morality. Unable to see, as Ramsay does, that this Old Testament standard only submerges all the potent turmoil of the emotional life, David shapes himself to be its lance in the fields of law, where the mind will triumph over the heart on all occasions.

His overriding preoccupation with the law affects David's whole world view and, combined with his role as narrator, means that the novel is replete with legal terminology and attitudes. Boy Staunton's final attempt to manipulate David is the clear rebuke administered by his will, which treats David as a trustworthy lawyer but not as a son. David reveals to Dr. von Haller just how precisely this hit home. When he begins to relate his life to her he claims emphatically that he will not attack his parent because as a lawyer he sees that "there is a statute of limitations on personal and spiritual wrongs as well as legal ones" and throughout his narrative he contends that he is presenting objective evidence. He argues that adultery by a man is more serious than by a woman. David does so by stating that society and the courts treat the man's adultery as a crime against property. He crystallizes his dislike of Eisengrim by obliquely accusing him (the lawyer in him makes a direct accusation, with its accompanying possibility of libel, impossible) of the greatest possible offence against the system of law, contempt of court.

87

He views the issue of the Staunton arms as a question of copyright, and justifies his anger at Denyse on this pretext. David dismisses Knopwood because he is a homosexual and tries to dismiss psychoanalysts as well on the basis that he is distrustful of members of such groupings whom he has questioned in court. Throughout his Zürich Notebook he consistently tries to show how fair he is in giving credit to Netty or Caroline or to his father's powers as a leader. Again and again David draws on legal terminology or upon what appears to be due process to lend objectivity to his personal perceptions.

The central image of the law in David's mind is Mr. Justice Staunton's Court, David's internalized procedure for judging his own acts. In it he stands as accused, prosecutor, defence attorney, and judge. He sees it as the due process of his "constant and perpetual wish to render to everyone his due," and in the novel he has sentenced himself to undergo analysis for his outburst in the Royal Alexandra Theatre.

Insofar as Mr. Justice Staunton's court is a metaphor for the examination of conscience that most men undertake at some time or another, it is no more than a formalization of the process from the particular viewpoint of David's profession. But there is an important difference which reveals the shortcomings of David's personality and a vital legal point which reveals a hidden secret of his court. The difference is his addition of the private parts to the Lion and the Unicorn in the arms of the court which David claims represent the addition of morality and passion to the justice it dispenses. What he does not see is his failure to carry through this element of his fantasy in the procedures of the court. When he describes the harsh Calvinistic tone of the Canadian courts, he is actually describing his mental court, despite his claim that he has changed it.

> But in Canada we geld everything, if we can, and dozens of times I have sat in court and looked at those pitifully deprived animals and thought how they exemplified our attitude toward justice. Everything that spoke of passion—and when you talk of passion you talk of morality in one way or another—was ruled out of order or disguised as something else. Only Reason was welcome. (p. 68)

David leaves no room for passion in his court whatsoever, and the brief that he presents to Dr. von Haller consistently clothes his reactions in forms which would be acceptable in a conventional court of law. He claims his evidence is entirely factual and as his own judge steadfastly refuses to accept extenuating circumstances for his acts. A court which could accept passionate evidence and consider the moral basis of acts would have to be redesigned completely in order to accept opinions and explanations which lacked the rigorous proofs of evidence.

There are then two serious flaws in David's procedure. First, if Mr. Justice Staunton's court really operated by the strict rules of legal evidence it would not accept the myriad of personal judgments of others which David offers disguised as fact and which radically colour his judgment. The most prominent of these is, of course, his concept of his father. Dunstan Ramsay, Father Knopwood, and Dr. Louis Wolff all attempt at various times to disillusion him, and in a court of law these corroborative witnesses would have to be heard. David dismisses them. Secondly, David assumes that the addition of privates to the animals makes his court an agency capable of judging the full human being when in fact it remains the domain of a strict and merciless code. He is attempting to force the world into the scope of the law to overcome his awareness that the law is not everything, but it does not work, and the limited perception of his professional training is triumphant.

The legal point which reveals the second key flaw in David's method is the McNaghton Rule. This formula for determining responsibility in criminal matters turns on asking the accused whether he would have committed the act had a policeman been beside him. It proposes that the accused is both aware of the illegality of his act and aware that apprehension and punishment should follow it. It hangs Jimmy Veale and it is expressed vividly by Don McQuilly and Bill Unsworth just before the boys ravage the summer cottage:

> "My grandfather's a judge," said McQuilly. "I have to watch my step."
> "I don't see your grandfather anywhere around," said Bill. (p. 172)

When it is viewed as part of David's metaphorical court the crux of the McNaghton Rule is its function as a representative of conscience. It is absolute. David knows the quality of his actions without the rigmarole of the court because he is his own policeman, always standing beside himself and always morally aware. Whether one calls this super-ego or a moral sense, his internal policeman makes the real decisions, not on the grounds of the law but on the basis of the confusing, undifferentiated mass of personal experience. David's near tragedy is that Mr. Justice Staunton's court sees the Rule invoked only once, in the incident which drives David to Zürich. Had he applied it to his tirade against Knopwood, to his father's actions, or to many other events his view of the world would have been quite different.

David views Mr. Justice Staunton's court as the cornerstone of his claims to a wholly sufficient self-knowledge. But the reader can see that this is an illusory claim, based upon David's ostensibly fair but in reality subjective perception of other people and events and upon the false premise that the court embraces all facets of human behaviour.

Robertson Davies' selection of a peculiar kind of narration and story structure effectively illustrates the shortcomings of David's view and reveals him in depth to the reader. The story structure is comprised of four elements: "Why I Went to Zürich," David's direct narration at the start; "The Zürich Notebook"; the dialogues within the Notebook between David and Dr. von Haller; and "My Sorgenfrei Diary," David's concluding narration. An initial question prompted by this structure is why much more of the story is not set within the Notebook (for example the entire "Why I Went to Zürich" section could easily have been incorporated). The most probable answer to this is that Davies wanted to impress upon the reader that David always displays legalistic attitudes, that the lawyer's utterances in the Zürich brief present his "complete" self as he perceives it. This explains why David does not adopt a different style or format for the brief but simply carries on the Plain Style of Ramsay and the courts. "Why I Went to Zürich" also establishes the framework for the legal brief by providing an external narrative to establish it. The "Sorgenfrei Diary" at the close of the book is an important tonic against the presumption that analysis alone can make man whole. Instead it points to the value of experience and social intercourse, and its contemplative tone offers a portrait of a changed David Staunton which could not have emerged in the Zürich Notebook. Its title, "My Sorgenfrei Diary," is an expression of David's condition after his year of analysis with Dr. von Haller. He has been freed of the cares which brought him to Zürich, and in the clear air of the Swiss mountains he is able to participate in a series of extraordinary experiences which he can, at that point, begin to grasp in ways that go beyond the rational.

The Zürich Notebook is a selection from David's accounts of his own life as told to Dr. von Haller. It comes after the sequence of events built around Boy's death so that it is a prolonged flashback. Any personal case history would be flashback, but Davies—through the metaphor of Mr. Justice Staunton's court and David's precise, orderly sense for the presentation of evidence—allows David to shape and narrate his life story rather than merely respond to the analyst's questions. Interspersed with the Notebook are Dr. von Haller's interruptions to raise questions and discuss points with David. In these sections vital shifts take place in David's personality as Dr. von Haller gradually has him recognize the difference between legal and psychological evidence and come to accept the fact that Mr. Justice Staunton's court is an inadequate forum for judgment of the whole of a human life. It is only after a great deal of more gentle preparation that Dr. von

Haller is able to launch a frontal attack on David's excessive rationalism when he threatens to reject the dream of the manticore.

> There comes a time when one must be strong with rationalists, for they can reduce anything whatever to dust, if they happen not to like the look of it, or if it threatens their deep-buried negativism. I mean of course rationalists like you, who take some little provincial world of their own as the whole of the universe and the seat of all knowledge. (pp. 186-87)

Davies' use of David Staunton as the first person narrator of *The Manticore* is particularly valuable, for beyond communicating the obvious intensity of David's crisis, the choice allows for the creation of a very well realized fictional world. David is a very sensitive person, and the sketches of human behaviour and character that Davies presents through him spring to life vividly and effectively. David is also very used to the minutiae of evidence and can legitimately notice details that reveal, whether they be Dr. von Haller's professional tricks or the tiny puckers of skin between Myrrha Martindale's breasts. Of premier importance, however, are the ways in which Davies can illustrate how David's rationalism, reinforced by his legal training, leads him astray in his perceptions of others and allows him to disguise his own flaws to himself.

The heart of the ironic technique at work through this "partially wise narrator" can be seen in David's December 18 entry in his Sorgenfrei Diary. There he pinpoints the source of Netty's attitudes:

> Thinking of Netty puts me in mind of Pargetter's warning about the witnesses, or clients, whose creed is *esse in re*; to such people the world is absolutely clear because they cannot understand that our personal point of view colours what we perceive; they think everything seems exactly the same to everyone as it does to themselves. After all, they say, the world is utterly objective; it is plain before our eyes; therefore what the ordinary intelligent man (this is always themselves) sees is all there is to be seen, and anyone who sees differently is mad, or malign, or just plain stupid. (p. 278)

To the reader, however, David has just described himself, for whole sections of the preceding narrative have illustrated his own blinkered subjectivity. At the point in the novel where David offers this exposition of human nature he has learnt a great deal about himself and one savours the irony only briefly until he actually identifies himself with the fault and its offspring, *esse in intellectu solo*. Through much of the novel he has been a "partially wise narrator" because he could show the reader so much yet fail to see his own biases in perception.

David is far worse at perceiving people than events, for the latter respond readily to the laws of evidence and his sharp eye. Central to all of his difficulties lies his misapprehension of his father's true nature. He turns on Knopwood viciously, and to a lesser extent on Dr. Wolff, Ramsay, and Dr. von Haller when they attempt to enlighten him. He assumes that being kept in youthful poverty and mistreated in Boy's will are due and rightful transactions. He is positively fawning when he and his father dine with Myrrha, although his reaction to his sexual initiation and his feelings at hearing Judith called a "little Jewish piece" do leave him with some doubts. But in sum David defends his father's reputation while the reader gets through David's words an image of a ruthless, even cruel egotist who sees his son as existing only to add to his own glory. Although David claims to have changed his opinion after his illness at seventeen, the very words of his claim turn upon him.

MYSELF: ... Oughtn't she [the dutiful Judith Wolff] to have had more mind of her own?

DR. VON HALLER: But wasn't that precisely your attitude toward your own father?

MYSELF: Not after my illness. Nevertheless, there was a difference. Because my father really was a great man. (p. 217)

David also fails to realize why his sister Caroline can upset him so deeply and manipulate him because of her remarkable emotional personality or how Beesty Bastable, whole talents David sees limited to "his damned bond business," can efficiently take care of Boy Staunton's funeral arrangements.

The most important errors in judgment and rationalizations to hide truth are in David's perceptions of himself. His treatment of Denyse is an excellent example of his mental strategies at work. Because he intensely dislikes the idea that she should marry Boy (one feels this dislike is firmly based on his desire for Boy's affection) he despises everything connected with her. But the reader is able to form two impressions of Denyse and in doing so comes to realize how David twists reality. The "real" Denyse is practical, effective, rather loud, tender to her daughter, and very powerful in a gauche fashion. David (like Dunstan Ramsay) sees only her faults, most particularly her attempts to remodel his father and force David into the mold as his father's son. David converts his dislike into action by having Denyse investigated. Not only is he looking for a legal reason to dislike her, in perfect keeping with his character, but he also holds up a piece of rationalization to justify his action.

92

DR. VON HALLER: You have no doubts about the propriety of that [spying on Denyse]?

MYSELF: None. After all, she was marrying considerably over a hundred million dollars. I wanted to know who she was. (p. 265)

The action of rationalization, of offering a justification beyond apparent reproach, is a classic manoeuvre of a person who does not seek the emotional basis of his behaviour but instead employs the intellect to excuse it. David repeats this manoeuvre again and again: justifying his alcoholism on the grounds that it is a special duty of the rich, justifying his dislike for Dr. Wolff on the grounds that he is a Jewish racist, justifying slapping Netty because he has seen worse beatings, justifying his distrust of Father Knopwood's distaste for Myrrha Martindale on the grounds that the priest is a homosexual, justifying his "lurking" to observe Dr. von Haller by placing it down the scale from spying, and performing similar mental acrobatics on many other occasions.

In falsely justifying his behaviours David reveals one of the most valuable aspects of the narrative voice Davies employs. David, the strict legalist with an absolute regard for truth, is actually inserting in his "testimony" a great deal of special pleading that would be wholly unacceptable in a court of law. By a delicate balancing in presentation and through Dr. von Haller's astute comments, Davies makes the reader aware of this duplicity. There are quite far-reaching implications in this revelation if one considers David's self-justification typical of the way in which contemporary man avoids self-examination. David's other "legal" misdemeanour amounts to nothing less than "personality perjury." Throughout the greater part of his account he poses as the slightly drunken criminal lawyer, a daring and romantic image. When Dr. von Haller finally raises the matter of persona David is prepared to drop his mask, but he could not have done so earlier in the novel. He has been so dependent on his image that he has been living it and drinking away the rest of his life.

David makes no effort to hide his admiration for the law, whether he is speaking of the ceremonial order of the Inns of Court or of his deep respect for its ability to render every man his due through process and precedent. His awareness of the limitations of the law in dealing with the fullness of human experience is limited to an intellectual recognition and does not penetrate the real roots of his personality. The reader of the novel is made sharply aware—through the narrative technique, through David's hollow self-justifications, through his excessive use of legal symbols, through Mr. Justice Staunton's court, and through his consistent use of legal judgments—

that David's world is not merely influenced but is seriously distorted by his pursuit of the law. His vision of the world is, in sum, that of the Old Testament or Calvinist judgment, where right and wrong hinge upon the facts of acts and where there is no room for mercy or passionate understanding.

The really important event in *The Manticore* is the expansion of David's view of reality and the subsequent changes in his personality. The forces that finally change David's life are all representative of those aspects of the person and the world which transcend reason and spring from the needs of the psyche. The process begins when David's emotional self drives him to Zürich and analysis. Despite his own picture of this as a rational decision, it is clearly an enforcement of the McNaghton Rule, for it is David's inner irrational self which forces him to admit that the depressed, alcoholic man who shouted hysterically in the Royal Alexandra Theatre is no longer able to gain approval of his psychic policeman. Despite his contention that Mr. Justice Staunton's court sticks strictly to law (thus reflecting his personal view of the world), his emotional collapse, a situation outside of the law, begins his movement to wholeness.

The event which triggers David's decision is as irrational and inimical to legalism as the application of the McNaghton Rule in the realm of the conscience. Magnus Eisengrim's *Soirée of Illusions* upsets David deeply for a reason he tries to pinpoint for Dr. von Haller: " . . . he was a con man of a special kind, exploiting just that element in human credulity that most arouses me—I mean the *desire* to be deceived" (p. 62). David's objection is very revealing, exposing his blocked desire to reach the whole of the imaginative and emotional life. In his judgment of the show he is actually upset at seeing something done by a powerful romantic person because he unconsciously knows that this is what he himself does without admitting to himself that he is primarily a creation of the combination of his own imagination and the imaginations of those who watch his career. So Eisengrim troubles David in two ways: in resemblance to the romantic persona which David maintains (therefore giving the lie to that persona) and in the offering of a world of fantasy and dream-like experience which David's rationalism has cut off but which is a necessary part of human reality.

Once in Zürich David comes slowly to grips with those strange and basic ghost images of human experience, the Jungian archetypes. As the Shadow, the Friend, the Anima, the Magus and, finally, the Persona emerge costumed in the personalities of David's family, acquaintances and toys, Johanna von Haller suggests that they could be flippantly described as the Comedy Company of the Psyche. For although they occupy the most serious position in human lives the archetypes are the players in a comedy if comedy is

94

taken in its strict dramatic sense as an action which leads to a resolution, an acceptance of the world and the self as they truly are. *Homo ludens* is involved in the fixed dramatic pattern of life and he errs only when he confuses the disguises of the actors, himself included, with their real functions. Dr. von Haller guides David to an awareness of the distinction between people and the roles into which he has subjectively cast them. In the process he learns of the inner, subconscious energy which has a major role in the game of life and which he has consistently tended to dismiss from his own perception. This, in effect, changes the whole context of life's "play." Dr. von Haller chips away at David's legalistic and rationalistic view of the world throughout his treatment, bringing her argument to a powerful climax when she insists that David accept the dream of the manticore in order to broaden his perception. (This passage is quoted earlier in the essay in another context.)

On several occasions in the novel Dr. von Haller describes the process of David's treatment in terms of the action of a court. She suggests to David that he write an account of his life in his own terms, those of a defence brief. In accepting David's world-view as a starting point she begins with his established personality, but she states clearly that she intends to expand his perceptions: "... I [Dr. von Haller] think Mr. Justice Staunton sounds a little too eighteenth century in his outlook to be really good at his work. Perhaps we can lure him into modern times, and get him to see the law in a modern light... (p. 78). Considerably later, when she is identifying Judith Wolff as an Anima figure for David, she states outright that the "court" is hers rather than Mr. Justice Staunton's. The courtroom drama of David's life has been vastly expanded by her skillful direction and the chief actor now understands his role much more clearly, free from the confusions among actor, role, and disguise.

As a result of the forces and events which drive him to Dr. von Haller and his self-searching under the auspices of her court David emerges from analysis with a new understanding of himself. Yet the changes wrought in him remain primarily in the world of the intellect, and it requires the important integrating events of the remarkable last section of the novel, "My Sorgenfrei Diary," to try him in the fire of physical and emotional experience. David begins his diary with a frank acceptance of his past and an awareness (prompted partly by Netty's letter demanding that he defend Matey) that he is not living by his new understanding: "All very fine. Not too hard to formulate and accept intellectually. But to *know* it; to bring it into daily life—that's the problem" (p. 279). Then coincidence, or synchronicity, brings him into contact with Liesl, Ramsay and Eisengrim at Sorgenfrei, where strong currents of emotion and events lead him to the remarkable incident in the cave of the bears.

David begins his Sorgenfrei story by a partial regression to his lawyer persona as he questions his hosts in attempts to unravel the mystery of Boy Staunton's death. But under the unofficial care of Fraulein Doktor Liselotte Naegeli and in the presence of Eisengrim and Ramsay he begins to open emotionally, bringing his Feeling Self wholly into the active centre of his personality. In Eisengrim he fully recognizes the mirror image of his own persona, for both men gratify their massive egos by performing miracles. But Eisengrim also illustrates how an awareness of the distinction between persona and self can make for a more complete person. It is he, after all, who in a rare moment of sensitivity granted Boy his innermost wish, performing through his persona in art a kindness to the enemy of his Paul Dempster self. In his confused admiration and repressed animosities, David has never made a comparable gift to Boy. And it is Eisengrim whom David sees as his mirror image in desiring people to "be in awe of him." Awe is a vital word in the final portion of the book, but from Eisengrim David grasps only what he had thought all along: that it is a quality born of illusions which differing magicians can control.

Dunstan Ramsay provides David with a different sort of wise example, for he has lived the drama and analysed the performance of the Comedy of the Psyche. His view of David's past accentuates the tension between historical fact and subjective meaning, so that he can remind David of facts or offer them in a gnomic guise. David credits Ramsay's improved personality to his illness and advancing age, but the reader can more easily credit them to the changes in David's perceptions and his belated acceptance of another Magus figure.

The events of the Sorgenfrei Diary can be accepted only on the romantic and fanciful terms in which they are offered unless one assumes that they are entirely staged by Liesl or by Liesl and Ramsay. The rush of needed experience for David simply exceeds even the accepted bounds of novelistic convenience although not, of course, those of synchronistic reality. Davies achieves a particular blend of the myth-dream and a surface of realism partly by having Liesl actually engineer all but the surprising climactic incident of her involvement with David. She launches further important attacks on the remnants of his excesses of rationalism as they speak together on the days before Christmas, reminding him that his lawyer nature brought him to Zürich and that life is the most complex of games. Life, indeed, is as complex as the five-leveled chessboard that Liesl and Eisengrim manipulate. In the most vital of these conversations Liesl urges David to accept the heroic challenge to search his inner self and laments that he has not felt deeply enough to experience the "very unfashionable, powerful feeling" of awe that might spur him forward. She opines that he might break through: "You might manage it. Perhaps some large experience, or even a good, sharp shock, might put you on the track" (p. 307).

Some readers have found the large experience which Liesl arranges for David in the cave of the bears excessively crude, a purple patch that cannot be justified in relation to the balance of the novel. It is clear that she deliberately seeks to give David an experience which will awaken his sense of awe. In the cave, "Liesl was in a mood that I had never seen in her before; all her irony and amusement were gone and her eyes were wide with awe" (p. 310). But although she prostrates herself before the striking images of the great human quest she does not draw David across the gap to intense feeling. It is only in the horrible, vividly realized moment of panic when David—his body cut, bruised, and stinking of its own excrement and his mind stunned by the sheer terror of death in the dark—calls from the depths of his whole self for the strength of his daring ancestor, Maria Dymock, that David breaks the shell of rationalism completely. He does not merely accept the irrational rationally, for that was already within his ken but was not adequate. In that awful instant, when two lives are put to the basic challenge of survival, David makes a breakthrough that begins the fusion of knowledge and experience.

From that moment until the last words of the novel the quickening of the change in David from rationalist towards whole man is presented in several symbolic actions and statements. From Liesl David gets an offer of that complete love, far exceeding mere sexual passion, that he could receive only as he becomes whole and abandons strict justice as a way of life outside the courtroom: "I mean the love that gives all and takes all and knows no bargains" (p. 316). David himself feels "reborn," and the reader is struck by the natal nature of his painful, sensual thrusting out through the mountain. Eisengrim's gift of controllable dice reminds David that an understanding of the inner self will allow him to play at life with an advantage. Liesl's gift of the watch inscribed with "Time is . . . Time was . . . Time is past" (p. 317)[2] serves to bring together for David his life history, his central concern for his father, and the vital experience of the cave where the past converged upon the present to give him a contact with his deep inner self. Ramsay's gingerbread bears of St. Gall and the accompanying legend proffer the theme of the entire novel: " . . . that if we are really wise, we will make a working arrangement with the bear that lives with us, because otherwise we shall starve or perhaps be eaten by the bear" (pp. 318-19). David has enlarged his universe, and been changed as a person forever, by the blinding insight of an experience in which his bear growled but did not devour him. At the close of the novel he is beginning to work out his own form of co-operation with his bear.

The law in *The Manticore* functions as a metaphor at all levels of the story. In the specific clothing of this fable of integration it expresses David Staunton's rationalist personality and vividly demonstrates (through Mr. Justice Staunton's eighteenth-century strictness) the shortcomings of his personality. But lest one should see it in an entirely negative light it should be noted that the law permits the best use of some of David's many gifts and that he serves society through it. We have seen why the law suits David so well and what specific events led him to make his choice. We have also seen how analysis combines with experience and action to bring about a development towards wholeness in David.

The fable behind this particular telling is that of coming to know the self and of using the knowledge to break the rigidity of the walls of our personae. These personae we too often unconsciously construct to be our total selves in lieu of the ever-changing, ever-growing reality of personality. As the reader watches David being brought to examine his experience, that person raises questions about his own perception of experience. In this context Davies' selection of a criminal lawyer must be seen as quite deliberate, an expression of his judgment that in the Canada, or at least the Ontario which is his setting, a legalistic, rationalistic tendency is uppermost among the directions into which personalities may become distorted. Mr. Justice Staunton's Old Testament Court is the epitome of the facts, law, and duty of the Calvinist perception of reality, whose practitioners are so often secretly proud in their wielding of power and authority, and who often submerge their own guilts by punishing others for them.

Acceptance of The Comedy Company of the Psyche can, in Davies' view, overcome the rigidity of the self symbolized by the law. The real ancestors must be found inside each searcher and their gifts will not necessarily be within the confines of rationalism and the law. But they will be great gifts, capable of lifting those willing and able to receive them, and able to make fragmented modern man whole again. Any man may see himself as flawed, but only in a courtroom larger than Mr. Justice Staunton's can he exercise those difficult, supra-legal privileges of mercy, humility, and acceptance of himself. And only when he has begun to grant those mercies by genuinely giving them to himself can he take his place on the bench of humanity and seek to dispense a broad and liberal justice which, like "the love . . . that knows no bargains," is far more subtle in its judgments than the word of the law, for it embraces not only what man does but what he is.

UNIVERSITY OF GUELPH

NOTES

[1] Robertson Davies, *The Manticore* (New York: Curtis Books, 1972), p. 175. All quotations are from this edition.

[2] " 'Time is . . . Time was . . . Time is past.' These were the words she and Eisengrim used to introduce their Brazen Head illusion" (pp. 317-18).

Davies and the Drachenloch: A Study of the Archaeological Background of *The Manticore*

Patricia Monk

The climax of *The Manticore*[1] is an episode in which David Staunton, Boy Staunton's son, an ex-alcoholic, and currently the patient of a Jungian analyst in Zürich, visits an Alpine cave in which he is confronted by the remains of a prehistoric cave-bear cult. This cave—to which I shall refer as the "Sorgenfreiloch"—is so conveniently located and its contents are so perfectly adapted to David's psychic need at this precise point in the narrative that Robertson Davies might be forgiven for having invented it all. It is my contention in this paper that he does not do so—that he introduces into his novel a great deal of substantial archaeological material pertaining to a prehistoric European cave-bear cult, but does so only after he has, by careful manipulation, developed the material into something which, like stage props or settings, is designed to look as plausible as possible, without being "true" or "real" in the most common sense of the words. This process of manipulation transmutes, as it were, fact into "pseudo-fact": something which is neither pure invention nor pure fact, yet retains enough correspondence with the latter to allow us to track down from the text of David Staunton's "Sorgenfrei diary" the general body of material Davies is drawing upon. It is, therefore, with the most obvious of his references, St. Gall, that I propose to start my discussion.

The town of St. Gall (or Sankt Gallen) lies just under thirty-six miles (65 km) east and slightly north of Zürich, in the northeast corner of Switzerland, and is the capital of the German-speaking canton of the same name (or names).[2] Staunton decides to spend Christmas there, away from Zürich and out of reach of possible messages from Toronto, and the town does, as he believes when selecting it, have "lots to see beside the scenery" (*M*, 243). This abundance includes no less than three museums: the Old Museum, the New Museum, and the *Heimatsmuseum*. In the last of these he might have seen the first, [sic] prehistoric finds from Wildkirchli...the Wildenmannlis-Loch in the Churfirsten...and the Drachen-Loch near Vättis.[3]

This collection was acquired for the museum by Dr. Emil Bächler, who was curator of the St. Gall Museums for many years, as a result of his own work as an archaeologist. He excavated the three sites in the early part of the century: the Wildkirchli in 1904-1908, the Drachenloch in 1917-1923, and the Wildenmannlisloch in 1923-1925. These three sites, therefore, are clearly indicated as at least the first to which attention should be paid in seeking the original of the "Sorgenfreiloch." In the course of this examination, I shall consider the three sites as a group, under the four headings of location, exterior topography, interior topography, and contents, comparing them also under each heading with the text of *The Manticore*.

The problem of identifying the "Sorgenfreiloch" with any of the three sites is more complex than it would at first appear. For although the location of each of the three may easily be determined from a map,[4] in the novel Staunton's trip starts not from St. Gall, but from Sorgenfrei itself, and Sorgenfrei's own location in relation to St. Gall is not immediately clear. According to Staunton, he and Liesl and Ramsay, in Liesl's sports car, go "dashing eastward from St. Gall on the road to Konstanz and Sorgenfrei" (*M*, 247). A glance at the map shows that, although the main road from St. Gall to Konstanz starts out in a roughly easterly direction, just before Rorschach it takes a sharp turn left to run northwest along the shore of Lake Constance to Konstanz itself. Since Staunton mentions Konstanz, it would be logical to assume that the party takes the left-hand turn before Rorschach and continues northwest towards Konstanz, but does not go beyond it since this would mean crossing the border into Germany, and Sorgenfrei is specifically located in Switzerland. If, however, the party turns off the Konstanz road to the left before reaching Konstanz itself, Sorgenfrei could then be located somewhere in the region of the town of Weinfelden. This would be the most obvious location, but I am not happy with it. The problem is that, according to Staunton's account, the party was "mounting all the time, and...the air was thinner than at St. Gall" (*M*, 247), but a topographical map shows that north of St. Gall the terrain flattens out towards the Rhine valley. Since the second option—to continue straight ahead at Rorschach—requires the party to cross the border into Austria almost immediately, this must also be ruled out in view of Sorgenfrei's explicitly Swiss location.

The third and last option, although the least obvious, turns out to be the most promising. Turning off the St. Gall-Konstanz road to the right before it reaches Rorschach would take Staunton, Liesl and Ramsay, along minor roads, into the northeast corner of the canton of Ausser Rhoden. The topographical map shows the area to be fairly mountainous; although we are not here in the high Alps, there are a few respectable peaks, such as the Gäbris (4,114 feet [1254 m]). This third option has the additional advantages of locating Sorgenfrei no further north than St. Gall itself, and much closer to the town than the Weinfelden option, both of which simplify estimating the distances between Sorgenfrei and the cave-sites. I am therefore inclined to locate Sorgenfrei somewhere in the region a few miles northeast of the Gäbris.

Such a location for Sorgenfrei itself would allow the "Sorgenfreiloch" to be identified with any one of Bächler's three caves with some degree of plausibility. All lie at varying distances, measured "as the crow flies," south of Sorgenfrei and St. Gall. The Wildkirchli is the nearest (10 miles [18 km]), opening "in the vertical walls of the Ebenalp" in the Säntis.[5] The Wildenmannlisloch (18.6 miles [32.6 km] away) is further south and more westerly than the Wildkirchli, and is, in fact, the most westerly of the three. It opens "in one of the rocky ridges whose upper edge forms the Selun summit which is one of the Churfirsten," a group of peaks on the north shore of the Wallensee (Sauter, p. 28). The Drachenloch (33.5 miles [60.6 km] away) in the Drachenberg is located "in the middle of the mighty, remote, vertiginous crags of the Grauen Hörner-Calanda-Ringelkette ... near Vättis, in the Tamina-Calfeisental."[6] Staunton's account of the journey from Sorgenfrei to the "Sorgenfreiloch" involves a drive of "about half an hour, uphill all the way" (M, 297). "Uphill all the way" requires that they should be travelling in a southerly direction, which would apply equally to all three caves concerned, but the limit of "about half an hour" opens up the possibility of choice. It seems to make the Drachenloch the least likely, since 33 miles in half an hour would suggest an average speed of 60 mph— which seems a little high over mountain roads, even for a sports car. My own feeling is that Davies has placed the "Sorgenfreiloch" at the Wildkirchli's location in the Säntis.

There is less doubt about the identification of the immediate topography of the "Sorgenfreiloch" with that of any of Bächler's three caves: the Drachenloch wins easily. The Wildkirchli can be approached without difficulty on foot from the village of Weissbad; the Wildenmannlisloch is in the Churfirsten range, which is said to rise almost vertically from the lake shore (Muirhead, p. 330), and no lake is mentioned in *The Manticore*.

The Drachenloch, however, is another matter. As shown in Bächler's photographic illustrations to his 1921 monograph on the Drachenloch, the

Drachenberg mountain, in which the cave opens and from which it takes its name, rises almost sheer to a height of more than 3,000 feet (930 m) from the floor of the valley. About three-quarters of the way up, the mountain splits into three separate peaks, the lowest being the Gelbbergalp from which the other two, the Vättnerkopf and the Drachenkopf, are approached. Although Muirhead classes the Drachenberg among "relatively easy mountains" (p. 333), and Baedeker merely remarks that "visitors to the cave should use due caution and bring an electric torch with them" (Baedeker 1938, p. 87), it is clearly quite formidable. Bächler himself describes it vividly:

> To go straight up the steep-sided labyrinth . . . is an impossibility for the average climber, for only the exceptional deerhunter . . . could get over the narrow ridges and through the fissures up the approach to the plateau of the Gelbbergalp which lies right under the Drachenkopf. (Bächler 1921, p. 15)

He goes on to describe how the Drachenloch is situated "with its high-arched doorway in the rock at the foot of the eighty-metre [262 feet] high east face of the Drachenkopf, the highest part of the Drachenberg" (p. 32). According to Bächler, the climb "from Vättis to the Gelbberghut took two and a half to three hours, [and] that from the hut to the cave one hour" (p. 11), so that a transport system of the sort described in Staunton's account in *The Manticore* (p. 268) would be entirely appropriate and necessary for the convenience of visitors. Moreover, to look at Bächler's photographs of the Drachenberg and the entrance to the Drachenloch is to see that the approach to this cave has a dramatic, almost flamboyant quality about it, which is very much suited to Davies' artistic purpose at this point in the narrative of *The Manticore*. In terms of exterior topography, therefore, I am convinced that the Drachenloch answers by far the most closely to Davies' "Sorgenfreiloch."

Trying to find the model for the interior topography of the "Sorgenfreiloch" among Bächler's three caves is disappointing. All three caves are simple tunnel-shapes, and one of them (the Wildkirchli) is literally a tunnel, since one can walk right through the mountain and come out the other side (p. 21). Maringer, whose book, *The Gods of Prehistoric Man*, deals extensively with the prehistoric religious sites of Western Europe, describes the Wildenmannlisloch as "tubular in shape."[7] The Drachenloch is similarly a tunnel which narrows slightly along its length and comes to a dead end after about 230 feet (70 m)—about half the overall length of either of the other two—although its entrance chamber is most impressive: it is "nearly 88½ feet [27 m] long , 18 feet [5.5 m] wide, and nearly 28 feet [8.5 m] high."[8]

The plane of the rock floor is horizontal in all three caves, except for a very slight downhill slope in the rearmost part of the Drachenloch. All three—Drachenloch, Wildenmannlisloch, and Wildkirchli—are clearly much simpler in shape than the "Sorgenfreiloch" of *The Manticore*, with its hidden entrance to a steeply-sloping shaft and huge inner chamber. On balance, therefore, I do not think that any of the three was the model which suggested the interior topography of the "Sorgenfreiloch"—although I think a model does exist elsewhere, and will return to this point later.

The contents of the "Sorgenfreiloch," on the other hand, clearly identify the cave with the Drachenloch. From the outer cave of the "Sorgenfreiloch," according to Staunton's account,

> all the sharpened flints, bits of carbon, and other evidence had been removed, but there were a few scratches on the walls which appeared to be very significant, although they looked like nothing more than scratches to me. (*M*, 269)

These materials represent the usual sort of archaeological finds, and, with the exception of the scratches (to which I shall return later), such evidence is found in both the Wildkirchli (described in Bächler's 1906 monograph),[9] and in the Wildenmannlisloch, as well as the Drachenloch. Bächler claims that all this evidence from the three sites shows not only a so-called bone-industry—the splitting and breaking of bones for tools—but also the existence of a cave-bear cult. His substantiation of this claim for the existence of the cult is the considerable quantity of cave-bear skulls, bones, and teeth found in the caves, although his interpretation of his finds has been disputed by other Swiss archaeologists.[10]

Certainly the cave bear was an exciting find. *Ursus spelaeus* (now extinct) was "about twice the size of our common bear (*ursus arctos*)—about 3.2 m [10.5 feet]."[11] This is the nose-to-tail measurement, and would give the animal a standing height of 12 feet [3.6 m] when reared up on its hind legs. It was an "enormous and immensely strong, shaggy beast" (Maringer, p. 31) and a formidable opponent for early hunters, although like most modern bears (with the exception of the polar bear, *Ursus maritimus*), it was an omnivore rather than a true carnivore. E. O. James, who agrees with Bächler's interpretations of his findings, points out that

> doubtless it was the great strength of the cave-bear that caused it to become a cult object at a very early period, and as this was likely to be concentrated in the head, it would be the skull that would be preserved and venerated.[12]

This basically was the interpretation Bächler placed on the evidence of the cave-bear remains which he found in the three caves:

> there is hardly any doubt that we are dealing here with the intentional accumulation of hunting trophies by prehistoric human beings—an accumulation which falls well within the scope of the primitive hunting and sacrificial cults which we recognize in prehistoric times and even today among primitive hunters. (Bächler 1921, pp. 108-09)

It is, therefore, entirely in keeping with Bächler's interpretation of his finds that Liesl should tell Staunton, "The ancestors worshipped bears" (*M*, 272).

Bächler's interpretation rests, not on the mere presence of the remains, but on the way in which (in the Wildenmannlisloch and the Drachenloch) he found them arranged—which must, he said, have been the work of human beings and for religious purposes. In the Wildkirchli he does not record any such arrangements; but in the Wildenmannlisloch, according to Maringer (p. 31),

> Bächler found a bear's skull, minus its lower jaw, but associated with three long bones, wedged into a wall fissure; this assemblage was covered with a protective limestone slab. Four hundred and twenty-five feet [129.5 m] inside the cave, five skulls minus their lower jaws were found, each of them associated with several long bones.

The finds in the Drachenloch, however, give real body to Bächler's theory, and Maringer summarizes them from Bächler's own rather long-winded accounts as follows:

> In the "living quarters", the excavators came upon a low wall, some 31 inches [78.74 cm] high, formed of small limestone slabs, standing between 15¼ and 23½ inches [40 and 60 cm] away from the left cave wall. In the cist-like space thus created they found a veritable store of cave-bear bones. What was most striking was the great number of skulls, partly intact, partly broken, often arranged in groups and, apparently, in the same orientation. In most cases, the first two cervical vertebrae of the skull could also be distinguished. In one instance, the entire posterior portion of the skull had been knocked away, and although a thorough search was made for the missing pieces, none was found. It follows that only human hands could have performed this "decapitation". The sides of other skulls showed traces of blows that were obviously of very ancient origin; two had a small hole on either side of the forehead. . . . The form of the perforations made it far more probable that they had been made with an angular instrument. . . . Close by the stone "chest" described above, they found a second one set in the floor, over 3 feet [91 cm] in length, width and height, closed with a limestone slab some 4½ inches [11.34 cm] thick. When the lid was removed, the chest was found to contain seven well-

preserved cave-bear skulls and a number of long bones. All the skulls were orientated with the muzzles facing the cave exit. . . . Section III [of the cave] brought still greater surprises. Again, the left wall had been given distinct preference. Six cave-bear skulls were discovered set for the most part in niches, some of them together with other bones. The skulls were all lying on stone slabs, bordered by other slabs, and covered with a protective slab. . . . The most remarkable find was the very well-preserved skull of a three-year-old bear with the femur of a younger animal thrust through the arch of the cheekbone in such a manner that it was very difficult to extract. Two long bones belonging to yet other cave bears formed a foundation. Here, then, primitive man had deliberately assembled parts of four different cave bears. Finally, in the terminal wall of the cave, Bächler discovered a group of nine skulls protected by stone slabs set obliquely against the rock. . . . (Maringer, pp. 28-30)

From this wealth of detail four separate points can be shown to be reflected in Staunton's account of what he saw in the inner chamber of the "Sorgen-freiloch." The first thing he describes is "a little enclosure, formed by a barrier of heaped up stones" (M, 271), which clearly represents the "low wall . . . of small limestone slabs" of Maringer's summary. The "seven niches" Staunton describes "in the cave-wall above the barrier" (M, 271) seem to be picked up from both the "seven skulls" found in the second stone box and the "six skulls set for the most part in niches" further into the cave. Staunton's attention is then drawn to the skull in which "bones have been pushed into the eyeholes" (M, 272)—clearly reflecting the "femur . . . thrust through the arch of the cheekbone" in what Maringer describes as Bächler's most remarkable find (Maringer, p. 30; cf. Bächler, 1921, p. 108). The same is true of the "leg-bones carefully piled under the chin of the skull" (M, 272), which echoes the "long bones [which] formed a foundation." So that what Staunton sees in the "Sorgenfreiloch" is at all points compatible with the archaeological evidence found by Bächler in the Drachenloch and with his interpretation of that evidence.

In summarizing my argument so far, therefore, I would maintain that, once my initial argument for the location of Sorgenfrei is established, it becomes clear that the "Sorgenfreiloch" has firm links with the work of Emil Bächler. It incorporates unmistakably some characteristics from each of the three caves described by him: its location from the Wildkirchli, its approaches from the Drachenloch, and its content from all three (the contents of its outer chamber reflecting those of both the Wildenmannlisloch and the Wildkirchli, those of its inner chamber reflecting most emphatically those of the Drachenloch). Only in its inner topography (its size and shape) does it appear to borrow nothing. Davies, it is clear, is not using any one of them as an exclusive model, but selecting detail from all three and mixing it thoroughly. But Bächler's material cannot be regarded as Davies' immediate source, since there are a great many items in Staunton's narrative of his visit to the "Sorgenfreiloch" which are left unaccounted for by anything in Bächler's work—such as the "scratches ... [which] looked like nothing more than scratches" (*M*, 269) in the outer cave, the complexity of the interior topography, and Liesl's speculations about the "ancestors" and about the nature of the ceremonies in the cult. I am convinced, however, that all these other items also have parallels outside the novel and are mixed into it from a variety of sources.

There is, to begin with, nothing in Bächler's work which will account for Liesl's certainty that the people who worshipped the cave bears were "ancestors" (*M*, 269). Bächler describes his findings simply as traces of a Mousterian culture:

> In the Drachenloch, as in the Wildkirchli, we are confronted with the fact of a primitive culture, which no amount of exertion can shift into either a pre- or a post-Mousterian period. (Bächler, 1921, p. 129)

"Mousterian" is the term for the tool industry associated with Neanderthal people, and it refers to the particular way the stone tools are made. The culture extended roughly between 150,000 and 40,000 years BC, through the later stages of the third (Riss-Würm) Interglacial and the early stages of the fourth (Würm) glaciation. Liesl's grandiose "not less than seventy-five thousand years ago" (*M*, 273) places the people of the "Sorgenfreiloch" more or less in the middle of this period. Bächler's attribution of his own Drachenloch finds to the Mousterian period, and hence to Neanderthal people, was supported and made more precise by later work: "A sample of the charcoal taken from a Drachenloch hearth, dated by C_{14}, gave a date of 49,000 BC" (Sauter, p. 28). This would date the occupation of the cave as having taken place in late Neanderthal times, and many physical anthropologists today classify Neanderthals as *Homo sapiens*. Bernard Campbell, whose interpretations of Neanderthal people reflect the opinion of the last ten to fifteen years, asserts:

> Until recently, many palaeoanthropologists regarded Neandertals [*sic*] as a brutish breed that at best represented an insignificant side branch of the human family tree. Only now is this misjudgment being remedied: there is much new evidence to demonstrate that some Neandertals, perhaps all of them, were our immediate ancestors.[13]

Clearly, therefore, Liesl's statement, which takes for granted that the bear-worshippers are "ancestors," is correct, although it need not reflect an informed position on this issue. Davies' dramatic need at this point in the novel is for "ancestors," and so "ancestors" the bear-worshippers become— with enough support from current anthropological theory outside the novel to sound thoroughly authentic.

Moreover, her projection of their possible ceremonies is also remarkably plausible, and clearly does not depend either upon Bächler or upon the lone tooth found in Switzerland itself. Although he insists upon the existence of the cave-bear cult, Bächler himself makes no speculation at all about the form of ceremonies which might have characterized it, so that it is not upon his work that Davies is drawing when he makes Liesl speculate that the "ancestors"

> brought the bones here, and skins, and set up this place of worship. Perhaps someone pulled on the bear skin, and there was a ceremony of killing. (*M*, 272)

Davies leaves a clue to the provenance of these hypothetical ceremonies in the "Sorgenfreiloch" by offering us Staunton's first vague assumption that he is in one of "those caves . . . which are magnificently decorated with primitive paintings" (*M*, 271)—such as, although Staunton himself does not remember their names, Lascaux, Altamira, Trois Frères, among many others. As Liesl states correctly, this art comes from a culture much later than the Mousterian; it belongs to the Aurignacian-Perigordian, Solutrean, and Magdalenian cultures of the second half of the Würm glaciation which are characteristic of Cro-Magnon people. Maringer makes a connection between the different cultures, pointing out that the Mousterian bear-cult seems to have survived into the later cultures:

> Traces of this rite have been found at different places, for instance at the Reyersdorf cave in the mountainous region of Glatz, in Silesia, which early Aurignacian hunters used as a shelter. . . . men of the upper palaeolithic continued to offer sacrifice very much as the Alpine cave-bear hunters of earlier times. (pp. 62-63)

In addition, however, he makes the point that the "hunter artists of the upper palaeolithic period sometimes painted or engraved pictures of the bear on cave walls" (p. 71). It is from such pictures that he draws some conclusions about the form of the ceremonies in the later cultures:

> Such works would seem to suggest a bear-cult . . . the ice-age hunters would have avoided any naturalistic portrayal of the bear because . . . they feared to call it by its own name; moreover, they would have dressed up in bear skins to perform ritual dances, and they would have had a special

veneration for the bear's head, or conducted special ceremonies in its honour.[14]

This description in Maringer appears to furnish the raw material for Liesl's notion of "someone pull[ing] on the bear skin" (*M*, 272)—a possibility which gains further credence when it is noted that immediately after this description (on the facing page, in the English edition), Maringer goes on to discuss "ritual bear-slaying" scenes, illustrating the discussion with reproductions of two "wounded bears" from paintings on the wall of the Trois Frères cave (pp. 72-73). A particular trend will by this time have become obvious in my contention: it is that Davies seems, at some point in his research for the "Sorgenfreiloch," to have either remembered Maringer's book from previous reading or consulted it, since in the book, in very close juxtaposition, can be found parallels to most of the information which is put into Liesl's mouth on the topic of the cave-bear cult ceremonies which she imagines were practised in the "Sorgenfreiloch" by the "ancestors."

In further support of this possibility, I would point out also that Maringer then goes on, in the course of his discussion of the sacred nature of the cave paintings, to discuss the complex interior topographies of some of the decorated caves. It is here, I think, that Davies may have found the suggestions for the difficulty of the route to the inner chamber of the "Sorgenfreiloch." Maringer stresses, for example, that "the greatest number of pictures, and the most important ones, are to be found in precisely the most inaccessible passages," and he mentions Niaux ("which reveals its treasures only after one has ventured nearly 1,500 feet [457 m] into the bowels of the earth"), Trois Frères ("a seemingly endless succession of passages and chambers"), and Cabrerets ("a labyrinth") (Maringer, p. 79). Above all, however, he also cites the cave of Montespan in the Pyrenees, perhaps the most difficult of all to approach. To do so involved its discoverer in swimming several yards under water along an underground stream (surely claustrophobogenic enough to suggest the atmosphere of the sloping tunnel of the "Sorgenfreiloch") before reaching an inner chamber, from which a lateral passage leads off a further 650 feet (198 m) into the mountain. At the end of this lateral passage, in the words of Sollas, who visited it himself,

we enter a little chamber—the "salle d'ours"—and in the middle of this, on a sort of platform prepared for it, is the sitting statue of a bear.[15]

Maringer, following the account of the discoverer, Casteret,[16] describes the statue, drawing particular attention to the fact that

the sculpture lacks a head and apparently had never had one, for the surface of the neck section was just as weathered as all the rest of the body and . . . showed no trace of having been broken. Between the fore-paws Casteret was able to make out the fossilized skull of a young bear. Evidently, the skull had fallen away from the statue to which it must have been fastened by means of a dowel rod; in the course of time, the wooden dowel had rotted but traces of it were still recognizable. Originally, there-fore, the Montespan bear had been a clay statue with a real, bleeding head. The bear's body had a number of round holes evidently made by spear or lance thrusts aimed at vital parts. (p. 88)

The tortuous approach and the final startling emergence into a sacred place are clearly excellent raw material for fiction, but since underwater streams cannot plausibly flow so near to the peak of a Swiss Alp, Davies substitutes for the stream the steeply sloping, narrow passageway down into the interior of the mountain. Apart from this, Maringer's account of Montespan and Staunton's account of the "Sorgenfreiloch" present a marked parallel in dramatic effect.

I am not, however, suggesting that Maringer's book was the sole source of Davies' information, but simply that it might have been the beginning. In his Selected Bibliography, Maringer includes Bächler's major publication on prehistoric Switzerland, *Das Alpine Palaeolithikum der Schweiz*.[17] This citation would provide an easy bibliographical route for Davies, from Maringer's summary to Bächler's own more specific account, and perhaps, finally, to the very detailed separate accounts of individual caves which I have cited in this paper. Moreover, I think this transition is more likely than one from Bächler to Maringer, since Maringer's book is much more likely than any of Bächler's accounts to have come Davies' way casually in his many years as a reader and reviewer of books.

Given Bächler and Maringer, one could account for the "Sorgenfreiloch" in its entirety—with two small exceptions. The first of these is the existence, in the outer cave of the Sorgenfreiloch, of "scratches on the walls which appear to be very significant, though they looked like nothing but scratches" (*M*, 269). They are scratches, in fact, such as are made by a cave bear scraping or sharpening its claws on the rock of the cave-wall, just as modern cats sharpen their claws on trees (or furniture). According to Burkitt, the claw marks on the decorated walls of the cave at Castillo show that

man seems . . . to have been decorating the cave at Castillo at a time when the cave bear used the cave walls to sharpen its claws.[18]

Since, as he goes on to point out, the cave bear "becomes extinct at the end of Magdalenian times," the presence of the claw-marks provides important evidence for the dating of the paintings. In the "Sorgenfreiloch," too, the claw-marks are presumably intended to be part of the evidence for the simultaneous occupation of the outer cave by humans and cave bears, although they have strayed in from a description of another time and place, such as Burkitt's description of the late Magdalenian. In my argument however, I will simply adduce their appearance as evidence that, since they do not make an appearance in Bächler or Maringer, there was at least one other source of research material used in the construction of the "Sorgenfrei-loch," although this was not necessarily specifically Burkitt's work.

The second exception is the reference to the cave-bear cult site near Hudson Bay (*M*, 272). Dr. V. P. Miller of the Department of Sociology and Social Anthropology at Dalhousie University assures me that such sites are confined to Europe and unknown in Canada.[19] The reference seems to be purely gratuitous—an attempt, as it were, to establish a Canadian connection. It is, therefore, the only piece of pure archaeological fiction in the novel, so far as I can determine.[20]

What I have been conducting is a two-pronged argument. First, I maintain that the archaeology of *The Manticore* is factitious. In the novel, a controlling dramatic imagination transmutes archaeological fact by selecting, juxtaposing, mixing, and elaborating it, so that it becomes pseudo-fact—a reasonable analogue of true fact—and in this form becomes part of the structure of fiction. Second, I maintain also that the material out of which Davies constructs this factitious archaeology can be determined with a reasonable degree of certainty to include Maringer's *The Gods of Prehistoric Man* and the work of Emil Bächler of St. Gall. The archaeological background may offer us some insight, therefore, into the novel; for by comparing the original fact with its fictional analogue, we can begin to glimpse some of the literary strategies by which Davies proceeds and about which he tends to be justifiably reticent. In addition, the archaeological material may have intrinsic interest for some readers. But at the same time, it is necessary to remember that this material is worked on and subsumed into the structure of a novel, and that the novel itself is more interesting and important, when all is said and done, than either the research that went into it or the process of its composition. The archaeology of prehistoric Switzerland vividly illuminates *The Manticore*, but it is *The Manticore* we must look at, not the source of the light.

DALHOUSIE UNIVERSITY

NOTES

[1] Robertson Davies, *The Manticore* (Toronto: Macmillan of Canada, 1972). All page references will be to this edition, cited in the text as *M*.

[2] L. Russell Muirhead, *Switzerland* (London: Ernest Benn Blue Guides, 1948), p. 308. Cited in the text as Muirhead.

[3] Karl Baedeker, *Switzerland, together with Chamonix and the Italian Lakes: Handbook for Travellers* (Leipzig: K. Baedeker/New York: C. Scribner's Sons, 28th edn., rev., 1938), p. 67. Cited in the text as Baedeker, 1938.

[4] A convenient map of Switzerland on a suitable scale is that in *The Times Atlas of the Modern World* (London: The Times Publishing Co., 1955), Vol. III—*Northern Europe*, Plate 66: Switzerland.

[5] Marc-Rodolphe Sauter, *Switzerland: From the Earliest Times to the Roman Conquest* (London: Thames and Hudson, 1976), p. 28. Cited in the text as Sauter.

[6] Emil Bächler, *Das Drachenloch ob Vättis im Taminatale, 2445 m ü M., unde seine Bedeutung als paläontologische Fundstätte und prähistorische Niederlassung aus der Altsteinzeit (Paläolithikum) in Schweizerlande* (St. Gallen: Zollikofer & Cie, 1921), p. 8. Cited in the text as Bächler, 1921.

[7] Johannes Maringer, *The Gods of Prehistoric Man* (London: Weidenfeld and Nicolson/New York: Knopf, 1960), p. 31. Cited in the text as Maringer.

[8] For the Wildkirchli, cf. Baedeker 1938, p. 77; for the Wildenmannlisloch, cf. Maringer, p. 31; and for the Drachenloch, cf. Maringer, p. 27.

[9] Emil Bächler, *Die Prähistorische Kulturstätte in der Wildkirchli-Ebenalphöhle (Säntisgebirge, 1477-1550 m über Meer)*, in *Actes de la Société Helvetique des Sciences Naturelles / Verhandlung der Schweizerischen Naturforschenden Gesellschaft* 89 (1906), pp. 347-420. Cited in the text as Bächler, 1906.

[10] E.g., Sauter: "Archaeologically speaking, Drachenloch is execeptional. There is no tool assemblage of the same type found in the other two caves [Wildkirchli and Wildenmannlisloch], though Bächler interpreted a few calcareous flakes as crude points. Man's occupation in this high altitude site is attested only by traces of a hearth" (p. 29).

[11] Bächler, 1906, p. 379. *Ursus arctos* is the European brown bear and is very similar in size and weight to the common North American black bear (*Ursus americanus*), averaging about 5 feet [1.52 m] nose-to-tail.

[12] E. O. James, *Prehistoric Religion: A Study in Prehistoric Archaeology* (London: Thames and Hudson, 1957), p. 21.

[13] Bernard Campbell, *Humankind Emerging* (Boston: Little, Brown, 1976), p. 293.

[14] Maringer, p. 72. There is, of course, a very well-known representation of "dressing up"—the so-called "sorcerer" of the Trois Frères cave in France, who wears on his head a mask with antlers, and round his body an animal skin with a dangling tail.

112

[15] W. J. Sollas, *Ancient Hunters and their Modern Representatives* (London: Macmillan, 1924), p. xxiv.

[16] N. Casteret, *Dix Ans Sous Terre* (Paris, 1934). Cited Maringer, Selected Bibliography, p. 207; text not available.

[17] Emil Bächler, *Das Alpine Paläolithikum der Schweiz* (Basle, 1940); text not available.

[18] Miles C. Burkitt, *Prehistory: A Study of Early Cultures in Europe and the Mediterranean Basin* (1925; Freeport, N.Y.: Books for Libraries, 2nd edn., 1971), pp. 199-200.

[19] Although there is still, Dr. Miller informs me, a considerable veneration for the bear among modern sub-arctic people in North America; the Mistassini Cree, for example, do not give bear bones to the dogs, but bundle them all together and hang them in trees so that the dogs cannot get at them.

[20] Since I cannot find any authority for the "remains of the pine torches still by the entry" (*M*, 271), which strike me, offhand, as unlikely, these may be another pure fiction—the product of Davies' eye for a dramatic effect.

Canadian Theatre in Robertson Davies' *World of Wonders*

Robert G. Lawrence

Robertson Davies' Deptford trilogy (*Fifth Business*, 1970; *The Manticore*, 1972; and *World of Wonders*, 1975) is admirable for the versatility with which its polymath author has used literature, philosophy, psychology, theology, hagiography, history, films, and drama to reveal and enlarge both his characters and his themes. As I focused on important aspects of the Tresize theatre tour across Canada in *World of Wonders* and studied the mind of a creative artist at work, I have combined two of my interests: Canadian fiction and Canadian theatre.

Davies' Sir John Tresize was modelled on Sir John Martin-Harvey (1863-1944), an English actor-manager who brought his company to Canada seven times between May 1914 and May 1932. Davies condensed elements of Martin-Harvey's last four tours (1925-26, 1928, 1929-30, 1932) to create the fictitious Tresize tour of 1932-33. Martin-Harvey was, like Tresize, a protégé of Sir Henry Irving (1838-1905) and had a long career (*c.* 1880-1939) in the provincial theatres of England, usually including an annual season in London. He was the last major exponent of the nineteenth-century romantic and melodramatic tradition in the English theatre; he produced and acted in old-fashioned plays like *The Only Way, The Lyons Mail, The Breed of the Treshams, The Corsican Brothers, The Bells, Rosemary*, and *Scaramouche*.[1]

Martin-Harvey was akin to Tresize in physique and egotism, and was also married to his leading lady, Nina de Silva, known usually as "Lady Nell." Like Milady or "Old Nan" in *World of Wonders*, Lady Nell continued to play ingénue roles until she was past middle age. Both Tresize and Martin-Harvey were made honorary Indian chiefs, both spoke to countless service clubs, read the lesson in Anglican churches, suffered from gout, had major internal surgery in Canada, and were served by devoted advance agents.

I have observed many other parallels between Martin-Harvey and Tresize, but my primary interest is Robertson Davies' skill in adapting a real-life situation for the purposes of fiction and in capturing varied characteristics of Canada and the Canadian theatre world in the early 1930's. It was the end of the heyday of the touring companies. Davies writes vividly about unsatisfactory conditions in the frequently scruffy yet pretentious theatres and opera houses, about the audiences and their hunger for things English, and about the Canadian winter, along with the conditions of railway travel.

Readers of *World of Wonders* will recall that half-way through the novel, in the midst of Dempster-Eisengrim's recollections of his past, Davies puts him in a London theatre context (pp. 162 ff. All page references below are to the 1975 Macmillan edition of the novel). Eisengrim tells of his having been employed, at the age of twenty-two, by the Tresize acting company in the autumn of 1930 as assistant stage manager, double, and tightrope walker. During Dempster's participation in a dramatization of Rafael Sabatini's novel *Scaramouche* (which the Martin-Harvey company produced in London in April 1927) and a revival of *The Master of Ballantrae*, Sir John Tresize decides to revisit Canada, where he had previously toured repeatedly and profitably. The novelist's shift of scene to Canada is thus wholly plausible and brings Paul Dempster back to his native land; predictably he passes through Deptford.

In terms of the central thrust of *World of Wonders*, Dempster's two-year association with Sir John and Lady Tresize contributes to his maturation, thereby linking this novel with the *Bildungsroman*; as well, Davies' memorable descriptions of the arduous life of a touring company in Canada, the loneliness, isolation, and cultural barrenness in 1932-33 make this part of *World of Wonders* at least a third cousin to the traditional "garrison novel." *World of Wonders* qualifies too as a *roman à clef*, although the Tresize activities occupy only about a third of the book. In addition, some readers may recognize real people in the tall Swedish film producer Jurgen Lind and the bald, fat English film director Roland Ingestree.

In Canada the fictitious Tresize troupe of twenty-eight performed 148 times in approximately five months, and the Martin-Harvey statistics are closely comparable. The Tresize tour began in Montreal in the autumn of 1932, with the presentation, during the first fortnight, of *Scaramouche, The Corsican Brothers*, and *Rosemary*. The company then regularly performed *Scaramouche* to Vancouver and back to Montreal, alternating it on occasion with *The Corsican Brothers* or—on the return journey—*The Lyons Mail*. In addition, Davies makes several vague references to *The Master of Ballantrae*, a play adapted from Stevenson's novel. In *World of Wonders* the Tresize Company reached Vancouver by Christmas and played for two weeks; here Sir John Tresize was taken ill and operated on for appendicitis, rejoining the company later. Sir John Martin-Harvey, too, had a major operation in Canada. His was in Toronto on January 19, 1928, while touring with *Scara-*

115

mouche; he rejoined the company in Vancouver. It did spend the Christmas season in Vancouver in 1929, opening *Rosemary* on December 25.

Moose Jaw, Medicine Hat, Regina, and Toronto are mentioned in *World of Wonders* as other places of performance, of apparently *Scaramouche* and *The Lyons Mail*, followed by a triumphant return to Montreal for a further fortnight. Roland Ingestree's sexual initiation was scheduled to take place during the Tresize Company's pause at Medicine Hat for "a split week," a Thursday, Friday, and Saturday, late in January 1933. The Martin-Harvey Company performed *The King's Messenger* in a one-night stand here on Thursday, February 25, 1932, but I have been unable to determine whether or not Mrs. Quiller was drawn from life.

Robertson Davies' Tresize Company returned to England in late March or early April of 1933; similarly, Martin-Harvey's tour of 1932 was his last abroad. He was then sixty-nine, and the Depression had diminished touring profits. In *World of Wonders* Eisengrim continues his subtext by describing his subsequent loyalty to the Tresizes, both of whom died in 1939. At that time Mungo Fetch-Magnus Eisengrim settled in Switzerland, to begin a new phase of his career.

Davies gives John Tresize rather a romantic death in the novel; he dies of a broken heart some months after being refused admission to participate in an all-star tribute to his late master Sir Henry Irving at the Lyceum Theatre, London, early in 1938. (Milady survived his death by "only a few weeks.") There *was* such a gala matinee at the Lyceum on May 23, 1938, *Here's to our Enterprise*; contemporary clippings and programmes indicate that Sir John Martin-Harvey's contribution—excerpts from *Oepidus Rex*, in which he had starred in 1912 and 1936—was deleted at the last minute, because of his tardy arrival at the theatre. Martin-Harvey survived until 1944 and Lady Nell until 1949; like Milady in the fiction, she suffered from serious eye trouble in her last years.

The preceding paragraphs indicate that Sir John Tresize and his company performed five plays during the fictitious tour across Canada in Davies' novel. The plays which Sir John Martin-Harvey brought to Canada on his last four visits closely parallel the Tresize choices. (Martin-Harvey's three earlier tours of Canada, 1914, 1921, and 1923-24, are not relevant to this study.)

Davies needed, in the interests of artistic economy, only one Tresize tour of Canada; thus he had to make careful choices of plays to accompany the troupe. Martin-Harvey could be more extravagant; he brought the following plays to Canada between 1925 and 1932: December 1925 - May 1926, *The Only Way, The Corsican Brothers, Richard III, David Garrick,* and *The*

Burgomaster of Stilemonde; January - April 1928, *Scaramouche, A Cigarette Maker's Romance, The Lyons Mail,* and *The Burgomaster of Stilemonde*; September 1929 - February 1930, *The Only Way, The Lowland Wolf, Rosemary,* and *David Garrick*; January - May 1932, *The King's Messenger, The Bells,* and *A Christmas Present* (a curtain-raiser to accompany *The Bells*). Almost all of these twelve full-length plays had long been a part of the Martin-Harvey repertoire, and he repeatedly brought established favourites to Canada. For example, Martin-Harvey offered *The Only Way,* his enormously popular adaptation of Dickens' *A Tale of Two Cities,* to Canadian audiences five times—in 1903 (his first independent tour to the U.S.A. included four Canadian cities), 1914, 1921, 1925-26, and 1929-30. Martin-Harvey's livelihood for forty years depended in large measure on *The Only Way*; his company performed it over five thousand times, approximately 220 of them in Canada.

One might ask if Robertson Davies needed *five* plays for the fictitious Tresize tour of 1932-33. The summary above shows that in 1932 Martin-Harvey carried across Canada only two plays and a curtain-raiser, well aware that the Depression, talking pictures, and the motor car were making significant inroads into theatre profits (*Autobiography,* pp. 439-40). (In *World of Wonders* Davies barely alludes to the Depression in either England or Canada.)

At first look it appears as though Martin-Harvey's actual repertoire for 1932 (*The King's Messenger, The Bells,* and *A Christmas Present*) would have served Davies' purposes adequately; it is, however, obvious that the novelist's primary need was to provide something for Paul Dempster to do, activity that would bring him into close contact with Sir John and Lady Tresize and contribute thus to his maturing. Davies held off the Tresize tour until 1932 in order to make Paul Dempster old enough to profit from the experience. Davies had put Dempster on the circus train in 1918 when he was ten and kept him in bondage to the *World of Wonders* for just over ten years, freeing him fully only after the death of Willard in 1930. Dempster-Fetch doubled for Sir John in *The Corsican Brothers, The Lyons Mail* and *The Master of Ballantrae*; he performed as both a double and tightrope artist in *Scaramouche,* and as a stiltwalker in *Rosemary.* (*The King's Messenger* and *The Bells* do not require actors with talents of this kind, but other Martin-Harvey plays seem almost to have been written for the benefit of Robertson Davies; in his youth Davies had seen the actor-manager on stage in Kingston.)

Because the five Tresize plays are now little known to theatregoers, it is worth saying something about them. I shall show, first, how they incorporate

Paul Dempster's skills; second, how they reflect accurately the character of Sir John Tresize—and at one remove Sir John Martin-Harvey—and, third, how they reveal something of Canadian theatre tastes in those times.

Of the plays which Davies arranged for the Tresize Company to perform in Canada in 1932-33, only *The Master of Ballantrae* was never in the Martin-Harvey repertoire, although two different plays with this title existed in the U.S.A., in 1901 and 1919. An American company brought the latter version to the Royal Alexandra Theatre, Toronto, September 22-27, 1919. In *World of Wonders* it was referred to and acted only rarely. Several of the things which Davies says about *The Master of Ballantrae* are entirely appropriate to Martin-Harvey's most enduring production, *The Only Way*, which the novelist does not mention. In *World of Wonders* (p. 239) we are told that Roland Ingestree's parents had seen *The Master of Ballantrae* ten times in Norwich, often enough to memorize it. This is exactly the kind of loyalty that *The Only Way* attracted. One theatregoer was reported to have seen it over one hundred times, another sixty-nine times,[2] and Samuel Morgan-Powell, the long-time theatre critic of the Montreal *Daily Star*, stated that he had seen it forty times in England and Canada. In the novel Eisengrim alludes to *The Master of Ballantrae* in terms appropriate to *The Only Way*: " . . . even I felt that in some way the theatre had been put back thirty years when we appeared in that powerful, thrilling, but strangely antique piece" (p. 233). Presumably Davies never referred to *The Only Way* by name in order to inhibit an immediate identification of Tresize with Martin-Harvey.

I cannot analyze *The Master of Ballantrae* as a play, but readers of Stevenson's novel (1889) will recall it as a melodramatic tale of two brothers who are rivals. Eisengrim's summary of the Tresize stage adaptation (*World*, pp. 222-24) is reasonably close to the plot of the novel. Both Tresize and Martin-Harvey had a particular liking for dual roles, variations on Jekyll and Hyde; Tresize played both the Master and Mr. Henry Durie. Davies modified the climax of the English novel so that in the theatre version Henry shoots himself instead of, as in Stevenson, dying of shock. As Eisengrim explains, this death scene provided a better role for Durie's substitute (p. 225). (*The Only Way* has no place for this kind of double.)

Martin-Harvey brought *The Corsican Brothers* to Canada only once (1925-26), but it had long been one of his standbys in England. With its emphasis on twin brothers who have a telepathic rapport, the play is unquestionably romantic. The author, Dion Boucicault, made it possible for Sir John to perform the roles of both Louis and Fabien by allowing only one at a time on stage; the actor cleverly illustrated their contrasting characters. At the moment when Louis is killed in a duel, Fabien, in Corsica, has a ghostly visitation from his brother—when a double is needed—provoking Fabien to go to Paris to avenge Louis' death. Reviewers commended Martin-Harvey's intense acting, his attention to staging detail, and the scenic effects (such as the forest of Fontainebleau—See *World*, pp. 260-61).

The Lyons Mail, in fundamentals little different from *The Corsican Brothers*, had been a major Irving production for many years (Martin-Harvey had acted the minor part of Joliquet, the village idiot, during his apprenticeship under Irving); Sir John revived it in London in 1927 and produced it in Canada in the following year.

The plot, based on a real mail-coach robbery and murder in France in 1796, centres on two look-alike men (both played by Martin-Harvey), one a bourgeois gentleman, the other a thief. Inevitably, the "good guy" is accused of a crime committed by his "twin" and is brought to the shadow of the guillotine. In the play, as distinct from the real event, the innocent Lesurques is freed at the last moment and the criminal brought to justice. A double is briefly needed in the climaxing scene, the only occasion when both men appear on stage at the same time.

In *World of Wonders* Magnus Eisengrim describes the play *Scaramouche* accurately and with much detail (pp. 180-85, 199-200). The plot centres on a young French aristocrat (acted by John Tresize) who, about 1787, becomes a revolutionary; in order to escape from his enemies he must disguise himself as the *commedia dell'arte* juggler and acrobat Scaramouche. Mungo Fetch-Paul Dempster doubles for Tresize at appropriate moments. John Martin-Harvey toured with *Scaramouche* across Canada in 1928, a year after introducing it in London. I have been unable to learn who played the part of Scaramouche in this production. Programmes and the *Autobiography* have been unhelpful.

Rosemary moved Martin-Harvey chronologically forward from a romanticized French Revolution, which he had found attractive because it provided heroic, self-sacrificing stage personalities to interpret. In *Rosemary*, a very slight play dating from 1896, Sir Jasper Thorndyke, aged forty, falls in love with a young girl, but after a few days of emotional struggle he refuses to tempt her away from her fiancé. The third act is set in London, the occasion being the Coronation procession of Queen Victoria, June 28, 1838.

Fifty years pass between Acts III and IV. Again the setting is London, now celebrating the golden jubilee of Victoria's reign. The street entertainment includes clowns, jugglers, and a stiltwalker (played in *World* by Mungo Fetch, p. 233). The aged Sir Jasper sentimentally recalls his lost love, fondling the sprig of rosemary which Dorothy had given him half a century

119

earlier. In 1929-30 Canadian audiences enjoyed *Rosemary* very much: it was "exhilarating," "exquisite," "refreshing," and—perhaps most important?—"clean and wholesome" (Vancouver *Sun*, December 16, 1929; Hamilton *Herald*, January 3, 1930). In *World* Davies refers to Milady acting in *Rosemary*; Lady Martin-Harvey was never in this play because there was no suitable part for her.

It is not relevant to write about half a dozen other romantic plays in the Martin-Harvey repertoire (listed above) of which Davies made no use for the fictitious Tresize tour of Canada. They are similar in character to the five which the novelist did choose.[3]

These plays which suited Paul Dempster's special stage skills were also appropriate for Canadian audiences of 1932. Davies refers repeatedly to their old fashioned tastes (for example, *World*, pp. 251-52); Martin-Harvey's sound instinct was to bring to Canada plays which had had an enduring popularity in the English provinces.

In *World* Davies writes of the large number of people with English origins in Tresize's Canadian audiences (p. 252); indeed, the novelist might have read the words of a Toronto reviewer: "A great proportion of the [Martin-Harvey] audiences have been British-born residents of the city" (*Star Weekly*, February 28, 1914). Probably this state of affairs continued for the eighteen years of Martin-Harvey visits, although certainly he could not depend on the British-born to fill theatres across Canada. Yet the statistics concerning English immigration to Canada during this period are impressive.

Between 1901 and 1931 almost a million and a quarter people migrated to Canada from England, an average of 40,000 a year to a country with a total population of between five million (1901) and ten million (1931). Another 400,000 or so immigrants came to Canada from other areas of the United Kingdom during the same period. Obviously some of these immigrants died, some returned to their homeland, some moved on to the U.S.A., and others were not theatregoers; however, it is evident that English men and women, and no doubt their offspring, could have made up a substantial portion of any Martin-Harvey or Tresize audience in Canada.

As I have suggested, several of the plays that Martin-Harvey brought to Canada were already familiar to theatregoers with English backgrounds. *The Corsican Brothers*, for example, had been a particularly enduring English favourite. It had been first produced in 1852, was a part of Henry Irving's repertoire for several years, and Martin-Harvey often revived it in England between 1906 and 1915. The play received an important lift from two Command Performances (June 26, 1907 and November 18, 1908) before King Edward VII, whose favourite play it was. Martin-Harvey chose this play for his Canadian tour of 1925-26, although as long before as 1907 he had feared that it was too old-fashioned for *London* audiences (*Autobiography*, p. 365).

In *World of Wonders* the novelist describes repeatedly the eagerness with which Canadian audiences greeted the Tresize plays, but, for the sake of contrast, he refers to "some fairly cool notices" (p. 251). Davies might, in fairness, have described how in fact audience enthusiasm was closely paralleled by reviewer enthusiasm. One may speculate on whether the warm reviews were prompted by a pre-existing audience approbation or if the acclaim of the audiences had its origins in their awareness of commendatory reviews from Montreal, Toronto, and London (England). Many theatregoers were no doubt predisposed to like the productions because Martin-Harvey came from England (*World*, pp. 252, 255). The frequent echoes of Martin-Harvey's advance publicity in Canadian reviews suggests a touch of diffidence and some awe towards the company and its productions; in small towns the reviewers may have been drafted for infrequent theatre duty from the sports or financial pages. A remarkable review of Martin-Harvey's production of *Oedipus Rex* appeared in the Victoria *Daily Colonist*, April 23, 1924. After alluding to the "profound" impression that the drama made, the baffled reviewer gave up and filled five column inches by quoting a letter by William Archer to Martin-Harvey praising the actor's 1912 version of *Oedipus Rex* in London. (Archer's letter was probably an item in the Martin-Harvey publicity kit.)

On average, Canadian reviewers of the Martin-Harvey productions in Canada were more generous than their counterparts in England or America. Canadian reviewers were usually undiscriminating, making little distinction between *A Cigarette Maker's Romance* and *Oedipus Rex*; they were often fulsome in their commendation of plays, acting, sets, costumes, and music. Indeed, the professional critics of sophisticated Toronto and Montreal were as extravagant of praise as those of Medicine Hat, Halifax, or Victoria.[4] Reviewers in England, the U.S.A., and Canada agreed in candid moments that most of the Martin-Harvey plays were trite and old-fashioned, but commended Sir John's acting skill and stage presence.

During the seven Martin-Harvey tours of Canada there were, as Davies says in *World of Wonders* of the Tresize tour, "cool notices," but the majority of these had to do with Lady Martin-Harvey (Miss Nina de Silva on stage, Miss Annette de la Bordierie in *World*). Most Canadian critics were polite or tolerant concerning her acting, a small number even enthusiastic about her as Climène in *Scaramouche* and Jeanette in *The Lyons Mail*. A few critics said that she had never been a good actress, some that she was often miscast, others that she hung onto favourite youthful roles (Mimi in *The Only Way*, Ada in *David Garrick*, Emilie in *The Corsican Brothers*) far too long. Davies writes of "Old Nan" in similar terms (*World*, pp. 162, 217-18, 225-26, 250).

In *World of Wonders* Eisengrim refers to Sir John Tresize's last tour of the U.S.A.: "It was more than twenty years since Sir John had dared to visit New York, because his sort of theatre was dead there" (p. 252). The generalization here is valid enough, although Martin-Harvey's most recent tour in the U.S.A. had been only eight years previous to 1932. It was still a painful memory for him. His theatre visit to New York, Boston, and Chicago had been a financial diaster (*Autobiography*, pp. 507-09), and he was indeed glad to return to Canada, where he recouped his losses.[5] Martin-Harvey was always baffled by his failures in the U.S.A., not recognizing that, for many historical and cultural reasons, American theatre tastes were quite different from those in Canada. Martin-Harvey wrote of "approval and warm commendation from the Press" in the U.S.A. (*Autobiography*, p. 509), but a sampling of American reviews does not confirm this statement.

This study has centred on two men, the one real, the other a fiction who echoes the first. Sir John Martin-Harvey is remembered for having kept alive the spirit of Henry Irving a generation or more beyond its natural life by his assiduous and sincere promotion of the romantic plays that appealed to nineteenth-century theatregoers and many of their descendants. As well, one must credit Martin-Harvey with having brought to Canada, by means of his frequent, extensive tours, culture and glamour, especially to those residents and immigrants living in or near small, lonely towns with a minimum of art, literature, and theatre.[6] Martin-Harvey, like Tresize, was conscious of a mission in this regard.

No doubt the enthusiastic acceptance of the Martin-Harvey plays in Canada (and the profits he derived) contributed to his willingness and ability to carry on with them in England. Each of the seven tours of Canada (1914-32) turned a profit, but the actor-manager died almost a poor man. I believe that in England during the 1930's he invested large sums of money in theatre productions which were not especially successful. Then, of course, that country was, like Canada, suffering from the Depression.

In Sir John Tresize, Robertson Davies has successfully created an interesting and believable character. The novelist's intentions were twofold: He needed a figure combining a substantial, almost heroic stature, albeit with true-to-life warts, and a quality of idealism (*World*, pp. 190-94). This man was to make a crucial contribution to the growth and development of Paul

122

Dempster. (One should not forget the humane contributions of Milady to the process.) In addition, the novelist needed a character like Tresize—participating yet aloof—to help to interpret the puritan, hypocritical Canada which Paul Dempster had left and which was still a part of him.

By condensing and transmuting the real into the fictitious, Robertson Davies has created, via a theatre tour of Canada, an admirable vehicle for realizing his intentions. For more reasons than are at first evident, the adventures of the Tresize Company in Canada provide an exceptionally lively and authentic section of *World of Wonders*.

UNIVERSITY OF VICTORIA

NOTES

[1] The period is covered well in George R. Rowell, *The Victorian Theatre, A Survey* (London, 1956) and Michael R. Booth, *English Melodrama* (London, 1965). The most convenient source of information about Martin-Harvey is his *Autobiography* (London, 1933), although it is prolix, inaccurate, and incomplete. Maurice Disher, *The Last Romantic, the Authorized Biography of Sir John Martin-Harvey* (London, 1948) is also useful.

[2] Unidentified English newspapers, *c.* 1913, in Martin-Harvey's press scrapbooks.

[3] Martin-Harvey's interests were not limited to Victorian romance and melodrama. During his long career he produced several plays by Shakespeare, *Oedipus Rex*, and a few twentieth-century plays, but none of these remained in his repertoire as long as those described above.

[4] Samuel Morgan-Powell, the literature-theatre critic of the Montreal *Daily Star* for over forty years (1913-53), was invariably warm in his praise of Martin-Harvey plays. David M. Legate refers in his autobiography, *Fair Dinkum* (Toronto, 1969), to Morgan-Powell's sycophantic relationship with the Martin-Harveys (p. 110).

[5] The American part of Martin-Harvey's first independent tour of the U.S.A. and Canada, 1902-03, was unprofitable. (He had earlier been in North America three times as a junior member of the Irving company.)

[6] Davies has voiced similar criticism of Canada of the past in his Salterton trilogy of novels and in plays like *Fortune my Foe* and *At My Heart's Core*.

DATE DUE
